# GIVING UP ON MY DOG

## A STRAIGHTFORWARD DIRECTIVE FOR THOSE
## CLOSE TO GIVING UP ON THEIR DOG

TED EFTHYMIADIS

TED EFTHYMIADIS

**Giving Up On My Dog**

*A straightforward directive for those close to giving up on their dog*

Published by Ted Efthymiadis
Halifax NS Canada
www.tedsbooks.com

# INTRODUCTION

I'm writing this book for the people who are struggling with their dogs. As a professional dog trainer, my phone is alive with phone calls from dog owners who are at rock bottom. Because time is very limited, I decided to write this book as a means to help struggling pet owners learn more about what they should do with their dog. Should they train their dog? Should they rehome their dog? Take them to a shelter? Or euthanize their dog? This book helps lay out the options for a struggling dog owner.

As with every training book I've written, I find myself reminiscing once again of my first dog Phoenix because his life has helped to change the trajectory for hundreds of thousands of humans and dogs' lives around the world. Had I not adopted Phoenix fifteen years ago, I never would have become a dog trainer. His disobedience and predisposition to aggression was the catalyst that inspired me to become a dog trainer. In the first year that I owned him, I cried so many times at the thought that I might have to take him back to the shelter. Luckily for me, I was as stubborn as a mule and would not give up on Phoenix until I had him into a dog that I could trust and enjoy.

After ten years of training dogs professionally, I've come to know hundreds of fellow dog trainers around the world who also share my unrelenting desire to help dogs and people, and many of these trainers have a story that closely resembles mine. A dog came into their life that made them feel like a total failure. This feeling of defeat or inadequacy is what drives thousands of dog trainers to defy conventional wisdom in an effort to save more dogs' lives despite increasing hatred towards some of the dog training tools that dog trainers use.

This book will serve as a guidebook for those that are feeling lost, ashamed, and without hope. If you are a dog owner who owns a dog that is out of control or dangerous, I'm writing this book for you. My books and video courses are produced to empower those who have lost hope. If you can't see the light at the other end of the tunnel, you should know that your dog can be better. Don't listen to the close-minded people in your life that are feeding your soul lies and discouragement. This document was written because I needed something like this book fifteen years ago, but the world was void of such a book. A book that would not only soothe my soul and calm me down, but also gives me hope.

My confidence doesn't come from knowing you, or your dog. My confidence comes from working with over 1750 people just like you with dogs as bad or worse than your dog. I have devoted my life to working with out of control dogs that people are ready to give up on. I don't train puppies, I don't train agility dogs, and I don't train service dogs or teach basic obedience classes. My 40-50 hour workweek is spent with people just like you who are struggling with their pet's behavior, and this book is the best chance that I have to help even more people. So, buckle up because I'm going to tell some hard to believe stories, expose some lies that you've all been told, and show you how to get a trustworthy dog.

If you are not willing to use both positive and negative consequences on your dog, you should stop reading this book right now. Pick it up again when you are ready to change so that your dog can change too. While this book does make some mentions of dog training methods and tools in it, it's not meant to be a dog training book. It's more of a book to help you make a more informed decision about what your options are with your dog.

# THE LIE THAT WE WERE TOLD

*A*fter struggling with Phoenix for several months, I called my local shelter where I adopted Phoenix from so that I could ask for help. Walking him was like trying to walk a hyena, and off-leash was not an option considering the several animals that he had killed in his few off-leash romps. The shelter staff was happy to refer me to a local trainer with 30+ years of experience. When I called his office, his staff was happy to sign me up for one of their classes. With an unwavering belief that this trainer would help me with my dog, I signed up for the training and began to learn things that would forever change my life.

EACH OF THE eight weeks was spent watching 30-35 dogs focus on each other instead of their owners. Week after week, the dogs would drag their humans into the class and then again outside of the class. The other dog owners were lucky to be pulled into the classroom directly from their car because I had been yanked around for the previous 60 minutes because I didn't own a car at the time and had to walk to the classes. 60 minutes of pulling to the class, 60 minutes in the class, 60 minutes on the way home. Thursday nights were a pain in my ass. A royal pain.

. . .

THE TRAINERS WERE nice and considerate, but never really answered my questions with an answer that would inspire hope or offering any practical advice. Each week we worked on things that were not helping the students with our actual issues. Now to be fair, I have to include that I had signed up for a basic obedience class. I was told by the staff that it would be a great place to start, and would greatly help my dog. After eight weeks of training things like sit, down, come, heel, my dog was no better on walks or off-leash, but he was a superstar in the classes when he had two pounds of cut-up sausages being stuffed down his throat. Phoenix was a smart dog and knew how to get what he wanted. He knew that I would run out of treats, and the moment I did, the bad behavior came right back. Of course, at times, he still wouldn't even respond with a piece of steak being presented in front of his nose, a problem that 90% of my current clients can sympathize with before they start my training.

IN A PRIVATE DISCUSSION with the head trainer, he gave me some basic tips that proved to be fruitless. "You just need to give it more time, Ted. Just more time. It will start to get better if you give it more time, six months or a year, and you should start to see a change." I had graduated from the class and was disgusted with the process. Our tutorial on leash walking was deplorable. "Lure his nose with that hot-dog Ted, and he'll follow along just great," they told me. "If that doesn't work, just make sure to stop every time he starts to pull, and he will figure out that he's not going to go forward if he pulls." The luring technique proved to be fruitless as Phoenix would just start pulling the moment that the hotdogs had all been eaten. What terrible advice. The stopping method was even more of a fail. It took me 45 minutes to get three houses down my street. Have you been told by a dog trainer that the stopping technique is going to help your 90lb Rottweiler from pulling on the leash? What a freaking joke.

. . .

2

AT THIS POINT, you should have an idea of how much I hated that class. Here I was with my dog struggling with serious issues that hindered my ability to take my dog for a walk, and we were learning how to teach our dogs to touch a paper plate with their noses. When asked why we were learning this touching command, the trainer had a very detailed answer ready to spout off. "Well, Ted, if you ever decided to become a photographer, you could have Phoenix touch the shutter button for you on command and take pictures for you." My eyes have yet to stop rolling. That answer told me everything about the trainer and the class that I needed to know. I felt like a patient sitting in a dentist's chair screaming because of my pain only to have the doctor suggest that we try aromatherapy as a solution. Never was I offered a more advanced class to get to the bottom of the issues nor given any tangible advice that would move the needle for my dog. My first experience with dog training was one that took hope from me rather than an experience that inspired hope.

WHAT TRAINERS sometimes don't realize is how many dogs they inadvertently kill by withholding valuable information from people. Here's what he should have said. "Ok, if you've tried all of these different positive techniques and tools, then you need to find a meaningful correction if you want your dog to stop pulling like a sled dog." All I needed was for someone to level with me. All I needed was to know that I wasn't a bad dog owner for thinking in the back of my mind about correcting my dog. All I needed was $25, and a trip to the local pet store to buy a prong collar and my leash pulling problems would have been solved.

THAT ADVICE WAS WITHHELD from me when I asked about other methods. Many dog trainers would rather watch a human struggle with back pain and frustration for months or years if they can avoid the hard reality that not all dogs thrive with a 100% positive approach to dog training.

. . .

SOME DOGS CAN BENEFIT from correction, and that doesn't make you a dog abuser.

HUMANS HAVE BEEN USING corrections for thousands of years, and so have dogs. Apparently, we humans in the year 2019 are so advanced that we can train any dog without the need for something that their own species has been using for millennia. The problem is that our closed minds result in millions of dead dogs.

AS EACH YEAR GOES BY, our western society falls even further off the deep end. In Sweden, you can be put in jail if you put your dog in a dog crate and close the door. Would they rather a 6-month-old puppy die after eating something while their owner is at work? At what point does love need to have boundaries? In some countries, it's illegal to use a prong collar on your dog. The very collar that helped my dog stop pulling in just five minutes after struggling endlessly.

THE NARRATIVE THAT we are told is that all dogs can be good dogs without any correction.

THE ISSUE that I take with that lie is that it puts all people and dogs on the exact same playing field. We must all play by the same rules, or we will be sidelined from the game. Is it reasonable to assume that a dog trainer who gets a Border collie puppy at 8 weeks of age should be able to train that puppy with exclusively positive methods? I would think so. Is it reasonable for a 68-year-old woman with a 105 lb Rhodesian Ridgeback to be able to accel with positive-only training? Let's be realistic people.

THE PEOPLE who own difficult dogs are judged by their choice of how they go about training their dogs in just the same way that a person is judged who are attending a 6-week puppy socialization classes with their 8-week old puppy and that's not right. The two things are just not the same.

WHEN PEOPLE in positions of power or influence over others judge them and demean them for using dog training methods that do not directly align with their moral platitudes, they often turn the dog owner against them. Over the years, I've met dog owners who have been kicked out of dog training classes because they told their dog NO in an obedience class. One of these trainers was disgusted by the level of contempt these owners showed to their dog that disrespected the dog owner by kicking them out of the class in front of all of the other students. Way to be positive... It's true that not all dog trainers are as extreme as to go to this length, but it does happen where I live. When extreme guidelines are imposed on the struggling dog owner, only one of two things can happen.

1. The client believes the dog trainer and follows the training protocol for years despite the unrelenting struggle
2. The client tells the trainer to go to hell and uses the trainer's feedback to prove them wrong, often resulting in the dog owner turning to the dark side (balanced training)

IN EITHER CASE, the trainer is left feeling morally superior, and the client is left without hope in the short term, and sometimes dogs die as a result. Neither of these outcomes is beneficial for the dog that is being trained.

*DOES POSITIVE ONLY TRAINING ALWAYS WORK?*
As a balanced dog trainer, I'm able to use both positive and nega-

tive consequences when I train dogs. In this book, I will not be going extensively into the science of animal/dog training. However, I would like to discuss some of the benefits and detriments of both positives and negative consequences. When I mention a positive consequence, I'm referring to giving the dog something that they like or need in order to increase the likelihood and speed to which they do a behavior. For example, if a dog is in the living room and their owner calls them into the kitchen for a treat, that dog is more likely to come for that treat than if they didn't incentivize with a treat.

The most commonly used positive consequences used in dog training today are;

- Praise
- Food
- Treats
- Toys
- Freedom

Clearly, all dogs are more likely to come to their owners if they are being incentivized, especially if the level of distraction is low.

WHERE DOG OWNERS get into trouble is when the positive consequence that the dog is seeking is coming from something that they do not have control over. The same dog that is obedient inside the home is now chasing a rabbit at the park because the positive thrill they are receiving from the rabbit chasing is larger than the positive they know they will receive from their owner if they come back.

THIS BASIC COST/BENEFIT analysis is another significant reason why millions of dogs die each year. Dogs chase animals and get hit by cars. The treat is not as yummy as the rabbit running across the road. Another common scenario that I see every day is when a dog chooses to jump up on the owner's house quests because they would rather have close access to people over getting a treat.

·  ·  ·

As you'll notice, all of the cases of bad behavior that I have mentioned in this chapter could have been avoided, right? The rabbit chasing down could have been confined to a leash, and the jumping dog too could have been confined so that the jumping would never have happened, but now we are unveiling the true problem. People have busy lives, and they get dogs to enjoy, not so that they can devote hours each day to training them.

Do I think that every dog can be trained with 100% exclusively positive methods? No. But in reality, most of them could be if their owners had enough time and patience to do it properly in a nonjudgmental environment. The average dog owner is lazy and doesn't want to put in the time that it takes to get these dogs to turn around their behaviors, which can take years to do with some dogs with behavioral/aggression issues.

It would be easy to suggest right now that these lazy humans should not own dogs, and if we go to that extent, you'll have to throw me into the lazy category too. Who the hell wants to invest years into stopping a dog from doing bad things? Especially when they can stop them in weeks or a month or two. Throw me under the bus and call me a lazy dog owner/trainer.

A few years ago, I went to a positive only seminar, and one of the trainers who was conducting the seminar was talking about training dogs off-leash. In a moment of absolute delusion, he mentioned how training dogs off-leash was easy. "It only took me 16 months to train my newest dog to be trustworthy off-leash, she's a hound mix, and these dogs are nearly impossible to train off-leash," he said as if he were a dog training God.

·  ·  ·

How on God's wonderful earth is it possible that dog trainers can be so out of touch with reality that they think clients are going to invest that many hours into training their dogs? The trainer works with dogs all day every day, so we can only assume that it will take longer to train that same dog if a non-dog trainer is training the dog.

Can we stop and realize as a society that the vast majority of humans in this world are not going to invest years into stopping one bad behavior in their dog. I've seen veterinarians come to me and ask me to do electric collar training with their dog/dogs so that they can trust them off leash despite the potential for the veterinarian potentially being fired from their job. These veterinarians would rather buy a bandanna for their dog's neck to hide an e-collar then keep their dogs on leash for the rest of their lives.

Routinely I have dog rescue people coming in asking for help with dogs that they can't place into homes because of significant behavioral issues. Despite their stance on the tools and methods that I use, they still bring in dogs for training that need help because they know it's what the dog needs. These rescues are funded by people who are against any negative consequences, and still, they bring the dog in for training because they couldn't bear the thought of having to kill a healthy dog just because of their behavioral or aggression issues. Many people who could lose jobs, lose funding, lose respect, change to balanced training because they have tried the positive stuff and it's not worked.

Recently I had a friend of mine call me and ask me how to use an electric collar to help his dog from chasing cats. I was taken aback by the question as this person is a well-known trainer in the strictly positive training community. He explained that he had tried everything that he could think of, and his cattle dog still wanted to chase cats, so he wanted to know how to actually get to the root of the problem. I applauded his open-mindedness and helped him fix the issues in weeks, not years. What the hell are people supposed to do when their husky wants to chase deer? Either they have to keep that dog on a leash for the rest of its life, or they need to come over to the dark side, but luckily for them, the dark side is heavily populated by nice people who will help them without making them feel inadequate.

IN 1998, Jean Donaldson wrote a fabulous book titled *Dogs Are From Neptune*. Despite being 100% positive in nature, the book is one of the best dog training books I've read to date. It's a simple read, with to the point questions and answers. People write to her for help, and she included the letters in the book and documented the advice she gave in this book. Think of it as a dog training question and answer book. In the book, there is a chapter that focuses on a question pertaining to a dog that is chasing ducks. Jean made some good positive suggestions and then wrote something that I commend her for. "Because I am personally not comfortable with shock, however, it does not mean that I consider it "wrong". Recalls often encompass safety and quality of life issues, and so, in my value system, lies in the gray area vis a vis use of aversives. I could definitely stretch and cook up a hypothetical case in which I might crack and advise a shock collar to install a recall. I don't blame trainers for cracking when they feel their backs are to the wall, and they must achieve a result to save a dog."

THIS WAS from what I can tell one of the few public moments of honesty that has ever been recorded by such a high-level trainer who is world-renowned in the exclusively positive training community. A delightful moment of humility and honesty. Unfortunately, the dog training world today is far more saturated with egos and fear-mongering.

FEW THINGS in the world are more abrasive than a human placing themselves over another because of color, ethnicity, or moral high ground. The moral superiority card is one that I believe is rooted in the core of many trainers who exclusively use positive methods because it's a form of control that fills a void in their lives. Balanced dog trainers, which we will soon discuss, are rarely known to lash out at other trainers or clients. For many years I've thought deeply about this topic, and I'm convinced that it's because balanced trainers have a sort of outlet for control in their lives when they are training dogs. If they are training a dog and have completed a solid foundation in training with a dog and the dog is not responding under distraction, they are able to use some negative consequences to create some urgency to the command.

Balanced trainers are in control of the dogs that they work with, positive based trainers don't have access to that same control because their methodology does not allow them to override a dog's behaviors, and thus, some of these trainers take it out on the dog owner.

Lack of control and agency can make humans act in some rather offensive ways.

There are some inherent problems with using positive only methods exclusively

- They don't work well enough with some dogs
- They take more time

Positive consequences increase the likelihood that our dog will do behavior and also increase the speed at which they do them, but they do not ensure that they will do them. Luckily for problematic dogs, some negative consequences can greatly help to offset the times in which your dog decides that they are going to ignore your command and chase the rabbit, jump on your grandmother or attack your cat.

IF ONLY USING positive consequences was always reliable, I wouldn't have a business. I wouldn't sell thousands of balanced training books, and I wouldn't be flown around the world to teach at dog training seminars for struggling dog rescue owners/dog owners. Positive is good for some dogs, but others need some negative consequences to get past training roadblocks. It's about finding a balance that will get humans results in a reasonable amount of time.

IT PAINS me to think of the millions of dogs that have been killed in gas chambers and vet hospitals because they were never granted the freedom that balanced training could have given them.

## BALANCED TRAINING EXPLAINED

Balanced training is the use of both positive and negative consequences in dog training to create a reliable, happy, obedient dog. Will they be happy 100% of the time, nope, but they will be happy in the long run. A competent, balanced trainer should do all of the initial training of commands using positive techniques to teach the dog the intended behavior. For example, A balanced trainer will teach recall (come when called) by showing the dog to come to them on a leash, incentivizing with a highly desirable treat, in a training area that contains a low level of distractions. When the dog is reliable in that stage of training, the trainer will start to take the dog to locations with higher distractions, at which point they will give them the commands again, and allow the dog to choose the treat, or choose to focus on the distraction. If the dog were to choose the positive consequence, they are rewarded for their decision. If they choose the distraction, the trainer would add a negative consequence by way of a training collar to decrease the likelihood of seeing that behavior (ignoring the trainer's command).

MANY GOOD BALANCED trainers will then give the dog a treat even though they ignored the first command in an effort to build a bond with the dog being trained, showing them that even if they don't do the right thing immediately, we still value the effort they gave us, despite needing the negative consequence to be obedient. Balanced training should always start with teaching the dog what we want the dog to do, then transition into teaching then what we don't want them to do, always ending with something positive. This is the true essence of consequence-based training, the dog is always in the driver's seat, and this gives them control over the training process.

THE MOST COMMONLY USED POSITIVE consequences used in dog training today are;

- Praise
- Food
- Treats
- Toys
- Freedom

The most commonly used negative consequences used in dog training today are;

- Head Halters
- Martingale Collars
- Prong/pinch Collars
- E-collars (electric collars)
- Slip Collars
- Social Isolation
- The taking away of something positive

# GENETICS

*U*nfortunately, so many people are without hope that their dogs are trainable. Six days a week, I meet with dog owners who are struggling with their dogs, and often, the owners will suggest that their dogs are not very intelligent. Many of these owners have previously believed the lie that exclusively positive training was effective with every dog, so it's only natural for them to conclude that their dogs are not very bright if they are still struggling after months or years of positive training. Most exclusively positive trainers do not tell their clients that their dogs are not bright. However, it's easy for owners to assume this when they see other dogs in the classes excelling when they are being put into a corner of the room to isolate the troubled dog.

I'VE YET to meet any dog that is not intelligent or less capable of learning to be a good dog. Surely some dogs are more physically capable, and some dogs are seen to have a higher level of intellect. However, these capabilities do not affect a dog's ability to be a normal dog. Your dog is not stupid, nor brain dead nor damaged, they just learn differently, and they are capable of learning to be a better dog if you will change your approach to training them.

. . .

MOST OF MY clients think that their dog is stubborn. Stubborn dogs are smart dogs, and they have just figured out that they can get what they want like a child who has learned to manipulate his/her parents. I always tell my clients that dogs couldn't give a crap about personal development, they are not interested in reading Tony Robbin's books. Dogs that are stubborn, disobedient, or aggressive very rarely figure out how to better behave on their own without some persuasion. My clients who own stubborn dogs are told to stop giving their dogs two options. If you give a stubborn or aggressive dog two options, they will always choose the option that makes you look like an idiot.

OK, let's mention a few scenarios where dogs cause people to look like idiots. Let's say your dog stops when you go for a walk and lays down on the sidewalk, unwilling to budge. Dogs do this because the owners allowed them to slow down in the first place. Fixing this is simple. Buy a martingale collar for your dog, this is just a collar that you can buy on Amazon or any pet stop that tightens when a dog steps back, so it's impossible for a dog to escape from. When your dog is on a walk and starts to slow down, speed up. Don't slow down when they start to slow down. If you don't allow them to flop down on the ground in the first place, they will just keep going when they feel the resistance on the collar when you speed up.

ANOTHER COMMON ISSUE that I see is dogs that don't want to jump into the back of the car. I always tell the clients that I will have the dog jumping in the car in 15 seconds or less, only to have them laugh at me. I put a martingale collar on the dog and attach a 20-foot long leash. If the car is a hatchback or SUV, I feed the long leash through the open gate in the back and grab the long leash through the back seat. If the car is a four-door sedan and the dog is expected to jump up into the back seat of the car, I'll fit the leash through one door, and pull the dog from the other side of the car. Every single time, the dogs put the brakes on and resist jumping in. I add a slight amount of pressure on the leash and wait for 10-15 seconds, and miraculously, the dog jumps into the car. The owners watch on in amazement as if they just watched Jesus walk on water, and I always say the same thing, "Stop giving him two options and start giving him only one."

WHEN WE WALK our dogs with dog training collars that allow them to pull us down the street without a negative consequence, they learn that they have two options.

1. Walk nicely with mom/dad and get a treat and a pat on the head
2. Walk like a maniac and have more fun

OFTEN TIMES I've heard dog owners suggest that their dog's genetics are the reason for their issues, and they cannot be overcome because their dog trainer told them that their issues could never be reprogrammed. Yes, genetics will mold your dog's temperament in specific ways, but training can override genetics if done properly. Frequently, I train livestock guardian dogs like Great Pyrenees dogs. These dogs are bred to guard property and livestock, so it's not a stretch to assume that many of them start to guard homes, property, people, etc. Yes, these are genetically motivated behaviors, but they can be overridden if you know how to do it.

OFTEN TIMES, I am able to tell what breeder a dog came from the moment the dog walks through my door, and I observe the dog's behavior, temperament, and looks. One local German Shepherd breeder produces very consistent dogs. They breed police K9 dogs, and much to my horror, they sell many dogs who get rejected to local people. The dogs tend to look similar, and all come in with the same issues from this breeder, resource guarding with food and bones. It's no wonder that these dog owners are struggling with these issues because most police K9 breeders specifically breed defensive dogs in an effort to produce more of those genetics, which can be beneficial for a police K9 dog to have.

GIVEN the fact that these dogs come in at 6-24 months having already bitten the owners multiple times, are they able to be trustworthy dogs? Sure, they are. These dogs have learned that they can get away with guarding without any consequences. Resource guarding is one of the most common issues we dog trainers see, and it's as common, and it is because of poor breeding choices but mainly because the owners don't know that they are making it worse. Resource guarding is also, by far, the most prevalent form of genetically motivated behavior that I see, but it's entirely preventable, and entirely fixable if the owner has an open mind and access to a decent trainer.

GENETICALLY MOTIVATED behaviors typically start at a young age, as young as three weeks of age, as far as I can tell. There is a difference between genetically motivated resource guarding and what I refer to as learned resource guarding. As mentioned above, genetically motivated guarding often is noticed at very young ages, and learned guarding often develops around six-nine months of age. Learned resource guarding, too, can develop at younger ages if the puppy has been deprived of resources at a young age, but thankfully this is not very common.

WITH LEARNED GUARDING, the dog learned that the simple act of growling leads to them getting space. For example, imagine a 7-month-old golden retriever puppy has a bone they are chewing, and their owner comes to get the bone from them. The puppy growls at them, and the owners back away by 2-3 steps and yells for their partner, "Honey, Roxi just growled at me when I tried to take her bone from her." This subtle misstep shows the puppy that they can control humans by growling. The act of jumping back and yelling in fear has proven to the puppy that they have the power to manipulate. Over time the behavior becomes more frequent and oftentimes leads to biting. The well-meaning owner then tries to trade the bone for a delicious treat but doesn't get to the root of the problem. Learned guarding is most prevalent in breeds that most people do not associate with guarding because the owners of these dogs are not expecting or prepared for their dog to start guarding. I see it most in golden retrievers, border collies, and golden/labradoodles.

GENETICALLY MOTIVATED guarding is also reinforced in the same way, but again it's often seen at younger ages, and it's much more intense as it develops. Learned guarding can be broken rather quickly with a competent, balanced trainer, but genetically motivated guarding keeps coming back if the trainer is not equipped to know what they are dealing with.

THINK of genetically motivated guarding as an appetite that needs to be satiated and learned guarding can be seen as a bad habit. Habits can be easily changed, and in their place, we can give them better habits. Most learned guarding can be addressed with mild correction, by just showing the dog that they are going to be given a correction for guarding, and they will not scare the people away. Genetic resource guarding also forms its own habit, but it's important to also show the dog that they will have to deal with a significant negative consequence the next time that they choose to guard something. My personal tool of choice for this type of guarding is always an electric collar because it's the only tool that can be used to correct a dog at a distance, while other methods need to be delivered in close proximity to the dog, like a leash correction.

IF THE GOAL is to show the dog that they no longer are able to control their owners by guarding, growling, lunging, or biting, the e-collar is the best tool as it places the power back in the hands of the owner, who can administer a negative consequence from a distance. In the genetically motivated cases, it's common to require 2-3 high-level corrections to solidify the process in the dog's mind and make the dog safe over the long term. With learned cases, I teach the dogs to drop objects from a distance, then send the dog to their bed so that I can pick up the object. No growling, no drama, and the human is back in charge. In just 4-6 weeks of training, dogs with both learned and genetically motivated guarding issues are able to be trustworthy around resources, even at close proximity.

MANY DOG TRAINERS completely disagree with this premise and refuse to work with guarding of any forms because they believe it's dangerous. In reality, it's not dangerous if the person knows what they are doing and has the right tools to get the job done. One of the most common questions that I get from trainers is, "If it's like an appetite, the dog needs to use impulse control to avoid guarding, and impulse control is going to fail at some point, so how will these dogs ever become safe?" This is a great question.

WHEN I WAS 16 years old, I discovered that I am lactose intolerant. My body is so affected by lactose (commonly found in milk products) that my body essentially shuts down at the slightest taste of lactose. The next 3-5 days are spent on the toilet, and my knees and elbows get so swollen that I can hardly move my body. Now that you know this about me let me ask you a question. If my wife brings home a cheesecake (my favorite dessert), do you think that I need to muster up a massive level of impulse control to not eat a piece or two? No. I need zero impulse control because I know what the next five days will be like.

THE NEXT POSSIBLE question might be, "If you are using negative consequences to stop genetically motivated guarding, or learned guarding for that matter, are you also creating fear of the person or the object?" If done properly, no, you are not. I'm not afraid of the cheesecake, I'm afraid of the consequences of eating cheesecake, and I'm not afraid of my wife because she brought it home.

ANOTHER GENETICALLY DERIVED issue that is very common is predatory behavior like chasing, hunting, and killing animals. When meeting with clients for the first time who have Huskies, Malamutes, Hounds, and Beagles, I always ask them if they want to do off-leash training. The number of Husky owners that completely write off the idea of training their dog off-leash is astounding. When I was picking dogs to use in a recent training DVD that I produced, I chose a Basset hound and a Husky. Every husky owner I've met will say things like, "They get their nose to the ground, and they are gone and won't come back for hours. The breeder told me they are impossible to train off-leash."

ASSUMING a dog can't be trained off-leash because it's a Husky is silly. I've trained about every breed on the planet off-leash without issue. If we give our dogs one option, how can they possibly choose option number two? It's not rocket science, it's called e-collar training. Whatever your dog's genetics are doing subconsciously, there is a way to work with them to get your dog to act the way that you require.

DON'T MAKE excuses for your dog because of their breed. Excuses lead to low expectations, and low expectations lead to owners giving up on their dogs.

# ARE SOME DOGS UNFIXABLE?

*M*EDICATING PROBLEMATIC DOGS
It's common to meet with dog owners who are medicating their dogs in an effort to control their problematic or dangerous behavior. While I'm not against medicating dogs for these purposes, I do have some reservations when medicating for behavioral concerns. No veterinarian wants to medicate dogs over the long term because they know that the medications often don't work as hoped and because the use of many of these medications can cause liver and kidney damage with long term use. When these dogs come in for training, I work with the veterinarian to wean the dog off these medications. 100% of veterinarians that I have worked with over the years have been supportive of discontinuing these medications if the owners have a solid training program to follow. If you are a dog trainer or dog owner, please do not take a dog off of any medications without consulting with a veterinarian. Cutting the dog off from these medications by the cold turkey method can have unforeseen consequences, and these drugs need to be weaned off over several weeks or months with the help of a veterinarian.

A FEW YEARS AGO, I worked with a client who owned an aggressive

Labrador mix. She had been to six different positive classes, and her dog was being medicated because of his behavioral issues. His leash aggression issues were so bad that the owner moved to a new apartment so that she would be in an area of town that had fewer dogs, which she hoped would make her leash walks less stressful. After two months of training with me, they were able to stop his lunging issues on a leash and even socialize with other dogs off-leash. Hunter was weaned off his medication with the guidance of his veterinarian over a 17 day period before we started training and never needed them again. Medications can be helpful with some dogs, but many owners report that they don't work for their dogs. Don't allow me to dissuade you from seeking such treatment with your dog; just know that they can be harmful to your dog's health over the long term, and they don't always work as effectively as dog owners hope. If you want to see a before and after video with Hunter, you can see the video at the link below:

https://www.mangodogs.com/videos/


## NEUROLOGICALLY BASED AGGRESSION

It's not uncommon to hear a client say something like "He's seriously not right in the head. I've had dogs my entire life, and I've never owned a dog like this before." While I sympathize with these clients because they own a very difficult dog, this is rarely, if ever, the case. It's human nature to diagnose ourselves and others when something doesn't seem normal. We need answers, and sometimes the best answer is to assume there is something clinically not right with our dog.

I'D LIKE to start by defining what I mean by neurologically motivated aggression, and I should say that my definition is different than the way some use the term. I define it as aggression towards humans or animals that is completely unprovoked and has no trigger. Let me suggest that if you think that your dog has no trigger, it's far more likely that they do have one or more triggers, and you just have yet to figure them out yet. Some cases of aggression have clear triggers that are easy to spot by dog owners and trainers alike, and other times, these triggers can be more difficult for dog owners to notice and will require the advice of a trainer to help diagnose and find the patterns.

NEUROLOGICALLY BASED aggression seems to be motivated by a chemical imbalance or a brain tumor.

I'VE EVALUATED ROUGHLY 2000 aggressive dogs in my career thus far, and I can think of only one dog that I would say had this rare form of aggression. The major sign present was that the dog had no trigger and would attack people or animals at a moment's notice for no reason. At times she would be sleeping, wake from her rest and viciously attack any person or animal that was nearby, and other times wake up and be fine. She could also do this even when she was awake, which made her incredibly dangerous. The owners were never safe. They were walking on eggshells 24 hours a day. After one hour of questioning, I could not see a direct trigger, and I remorsefully suggested that the owner put her dog to sleep.

ONCE AGAIN, I need to emphasize how incredibly rare this type of aggression is. 1/2000=0.0005% of aggressive dogs that I have met in person have this type of aggression, that as far as I can tell has no cure. I suggest that there is no cure because current medications don't seem to work with these cases. To that point, I don't believe that training would help because it doesn't seem that the dog has the ability to start or stop their aggressive outbursts. If a dog is not choosing to act aggressively, I don't see how I could ever make that dog safe to be around. I'm a dog trainer, not a God.

CASES like this are often misdiagnosed when dogs fall asleep and then wake up and attack someone who has touched them when they were sleeping and woke them from their slumber. Those cases are actually possible to rehabilitate. I worked with a massive livestock guardian breed that was like this a few years ago, and we were able to stop him from acting this way by use of a muzzle and e-collar. Of course, he also showed plenty of other indications that his issue was not neurologically based or tumor based because he would attack when being woken from sleep, and was also human aggressive to people who came to the owner's home, which indicated that he was choosing to act aggressively.

RECENTLY I WORKED with a dog that was misdiagnosed with neurologically motivated aggression. It was suggested that she should be put to sleep by several professionals, including the shelter who adopted her out. She would attack the owners frequently, and luckily for them, she only weighed about 30lbs. After just 10 minutes of talking with the owner, we figured out all of the triggers and started training. Her patterns were actually very easy to figure out, but often dog owners are so convinced that it's a neurologically motivated type of aggression that they can't see the situation objectively. If you think that your dog has this type of aggression, I would suggest that you start by calling dog trainers in your area to get opinions. Call a minimum of 10-15 trainers before you lose hope and resolve to believe that your dog has an extremely rare form of untreatable aggression. Remember, it's extremely rare that you own the 0.0005% dog.

## MEDICAL REASONS FOR AGGRESSION

Some vets, trainers, and behaviorists believe that most or all cases of aggression seen in dogs are related to medical concerns or chemical imbalances. Not being a science nut, I always approached the situation from a completely different angle because of the training that I was given early in my career. My mentor never really focused on eliminating medical concerns before starting training, and I watched him rehabilitate hundreds of dogs without having the owners look for health issues. Watching this formed the way that I looked at aggression as a young trainer.

I SAW aggression to be a behavioral pattern that should be fixed with training, not medications.

IN 2013, I attended a dog training seminar, which was led by a trainer that I deeply respect who started to open my eyes to some things that I might have missed. I was very successful in rehabilitating aggressive dogs, so I thought that training was always the answer. In full transparency, my views have not changed on the topic much since 2013, but I am slightly more open to exploring potential medical concerns like thyroid issues, brain tumors, and pain issues.

WHILE I THINK that medical concerns can affect how a dog behaves, I also think that some trainers take the medical stuff to an extreme. Assuming aggressive dogs have a medical issue can be problematic because it often gives the dog owners hope that if there is an underlying medical condition, it will be fixed with surgery or a pill. This is rarely, if ever, the case. I've sent hundreds of aggressive dogs for full medical checks and had less than a half dozen comes back with any medical irregularities. And when the medical issues are addressed, the issues don't seem to go away. So, if you are going to invest the time and money into medical diagnostics, you should have very clear expectations. Assume that if they do find any medical issues, a pill is not going to fix the issue, extensive training will.

IF YOU WANT to do medical diagnostics, talk to your vet. Personally, I suggest a full blood workup and a thyroid blood panel. A thyroid panel is the first thing that I like to have checked because under and overactive thyroids can make dogs of all ages change their behavior rather rapidly in undesirable ways. In short, thyroid issues can make dogs more irritable. If you want to spend the extra money, have your vet draw the blood and send it to Dr. Jean Dodds at www.hemo-pet.org.

IF YOU ARE CONVINCED that your dog has neurologically-based aggression and that your dog is in the 0.0005% of dogs who do, I would ask your vet to check for brain tumors. I know several trainers who have worked with dogs that were suffering from substantial brain tumors who were exhibiting random aggressive outbursts that were so extreme that people and dogs were almost killed by these dogs. Unfortunately, all of those dogs died within a week of the tumors were found.

# NOT ALLOWING YOUR DOG TO BE DANGEROUS

*T*he single largest reason why people are attacked by dogs is humans trust dogs too much and let their guards down with dogs that are not yet worthy of unwavering trust. Because people love their dogs as much as they do, it can be hard for them to restrict their dogs' freedom at times. This blind spot shows up every single day in my email inbox as I get emails from loving dog owners who say things like, "But he's such a good boy 95% of the time, I can't understand why he bit my sister yesterday."

Granting an untrustworthy dog or new dog freedom because we feel bad about their lack of freedom makes up the lion's share of human attacks and dog attacks in North America each year. Don't put your dog is potentially compromising situations that could lead to your dog being put to sleep.

In North America, the number of dog bites each year is staggering and only getting worse because of loving humans who do not properly contain their dogs. According to a study from the Center for Disease Control, approximately 4.7 million dog bites occur in the United States each year, and 800,000 of those bites result in medical care. It's my view that at least 95% of those bites are absolutely preventable if people would be more diligent about safety and keeping others safe.

I HAVE aggressive dogs come onto my property every day for training and have never had a person or dog be attacked because I'm more focused on the safety of others than I am on the freedom of the dog in question. Each owner is required to wait in their car with the windows rolled up when they come onto my property until I come out and get them. The owners are then given a slip collar or martingale collar and a leash is put on their dog to ensure they cannot back out of their loosely fitted collar or harness. Under no circumstances do I allow dogs to run around inside my facility off-leash until they are far along into the training process. The dog's freedom or happiness is not my concern in the beginning stages of training. If I allow my clients dogs unearned freedom, that freedom could be the final nail in the coffin for that dog.

IF YOU ARE MAKING excuses for your dog, stop. If you ever find yourself justifying anything that you are doing by saying to yourself, "I know I shouldn't, but he needs the exercise," please stop. The number of dogs that are euthanized because their loving owners couldn't tell them NO is astronomical.

TWO YEARS AGO, I got a call from a man who was asking if I could meet him and his dog for some advice. He mentioned that there was an incident that happened a few nights earlier that he wanted to talk about. He went on to tell me how he had taken his nine-year-old son to the hospital who needed twelve stitches on his face. I then asked the father if he could elaborate further and tell me where the child was when the dog bit him in the face. He was completely perplexed by the fact that I was insinuating that the dog had bitten his child. He told me that the dog did not bite his child, what happened was that his son got out of bed to give his dog a hug goodnight before going to bed

27

for the night. It was at that point that his dog must have been startled and moved his head quickly, at which point his teeth must have accidentally grazed the boy's face by pure accident.

IT WAS at that moment that I realized just how delusional this man was, and I resolved myself to be very upfront with him in an effort to try to snap him out of it. I told him that he was lying to himself and that the dog had bitten his son on the face. Despite my critical attitude, he was unfazed and insisted that I was welcome to my opinion but that I was wrong about his dog. "My dog loves my kids. He would never do something like that." Despite not believing me, he still wanted to set up a time to meet because he thought that he should learn how to teach his dog to be gentler when being hugged so that such an accident would never happen again. We booked a time for him to come over at the end of the week, and I told him that if he wanted to meet with me, he would have to make sure that the dog did not have any access at all with his children before we were to meet. He agreed and thanked me for my time.

LESS THAN 24 hours after talking to the father, I got another phone call from him. He was absolutely losing his mind. "Oh my God, you were right! Oh my God, what am I going to do?" I asked him what happened, and his answer was not what I had been hoping to hear. "It happened again. I can't believe I allowed it to happen again," he yelled over the phone. "What do you mean it happened again? How the hell did it happen again? I told you not to let the dog anywhere near your kids. What part of don't let the dog near your kids did you not understand?" I responded.

"MY SON WAS SITTING on the couch watching TV with our dog, he was eating popcorn, and after he dropped a few pieces on the sofa next to him, our dog went for the pieces of popcorn and bit him in the face before I had time to grab my dog." My heart went out to the man even though he had made a critical mistake. A mistake that he will never be able to forgive himself for. He canceled our meeting and told me that he was going to put his dog to sleep that very day. I never heard from that man ever again, but I tell his story often with the hopes that someone will hear it and wake up from the delusional state they might be living in. Don't be like this father. Dogs are predators, and every one of them can bite, even your best friend.

# WHAT'S THE FIRST STEP?

*T*he first step in changing is recognizing that you have a problem on your hands. Remind yourself with each passing hour that time is not on your side. Dogs don't magically get better. They don't work out their issues with quiet time and wake up from a nap with a fresh outlook on life. You will need to prevent them from doing dangerous things that could get them in trouble.

TOUGH QUESTIONS ARE one of the best ways for us to get a more rational view of the situation, so let's dive in;

- Has my dog bitten a human for any reason? Y/N
- Has my dog attacked another dog for any reason? Y/N
- Has my dog ever gotten out of your home by accident? Y/N
- Do I ever make excuses for my dog, or give my dog unearned freedom because I feel bad for him/her? Y/N
- What is the likelihood that my dog will bite another person? ___/10
- What is the likelihood that my dog will bite someone in our family? ___/10

- What is the likelihood that my dog will get out of my home again? ___/10
- If my dog has bitten a person, what was the severity of the bite? ___/10
- If my dog has bitten a person, was the bite a single bite with the dog then running away, or did the dog continue to try and bite the person? ___/10
- Do you have any history with local animal control because of your dog's behavior? Y/N
- Do you think that your dog's issues are likely to get better on their own, stay the same, or get worse over time if you don't do something proactive? Y/N

WE ALL KNOW that we need to do something, but it's easier to put it off until tomorrow. Why do you think that we have to pay our taxes each year by a specific date? The due date keeps us accountable, that's why. Take some time now to answer the above questions with your family, no need to discuss what you will do about the situation just yet that will come in a later chapter.

WHEN PEOPLE ASK for help with their dangerous dog, they are often surprised when I suggest they keep their dog on a leash, or away from other dogs, or people. Recently I had a woman call me about her dog that was human aggressive and had bitten several people. When asking her how she exercised her dog, she told me that she takes her dog to a local park and lets him run off-leash. "He's fine with other dogs, and I just tell people not to look at him, talk to him, or try and touch him." It was clear that this well-meaning woman was not thinking clearly, so I asked her if she had ever had the pleasure of driving a car with brakes that only worked 98% of the time. "Would you drive a car if you knew that 2% of the time, the brakes would fail to stop the car?" I asked her. "Well, no, of course not," I told her that what she was doing with her dog was not any different. She could cost her dog his life all for the sake of off-leash freedom.

OFTEN, I will suggest the limiting of a dog's freedom before something serious can be done, and often it's met with pushback from dog owners because my suggestion will limit their dog's freedom and enjoyment of life for a short time. I've always found it interesting that most people will force their dog to submit to bed rest for two weeks after a spay or neuter operation, yet often will resist limiting freedom for reasons that might save their life.

IF YOU OWN A DANGEROUS DOG, and you are making excuses for them, know that you might be the reason that your dog gets put to sleep. A hard pill to swallow, but one that you might have to ingest if you allow your dog too much freedom, and it results in a dog fight or dog bite.

# A DOG TRAINER OR A BEHAVIORIST?

*S*ome dog trainers are great general dog trainers, and some are specialists, much like in the human medical field. Some dog trainers work full time with dogs, some part-time. Some are self-taught, some have apprenticed under more senior trainers, and some went to a dog training school. Some consider themselves a professional after reading a few books, and others only use the term after decades of hands-on experience. About the only thing that all of the trainers have in common is that they help dogs change their behavior. Dog training is not a regulated field, so you'll have to do some research to find a good trainer that will help you with your dog.

LET'S take a look at some of the different types of trainers who work with pet dogs;

- Obedience trainers
- Behaviorists
- Real-world trainers

MOST DOG TRAINERS are considered obedience trainers, which means that they train dogs to do specific commands like come, sit, heel, down, and stay. Most of the dogs trained in North America each year go through this type of training, and often, it's in a group format. While obedience training can be very helpful when added to the life of any dog, it typically is not something that will completely change the life of the dog that is being trained if they already have developed some extreme behavioral issues. For obvious reasons, dangerous dogs should not be put into a group environment until they are made to be safe. If they are put into a group class straight away, the owners, the trainer, and the dog will be too stressed to learn. Group training is not at all a bad thing, in fact, problematic dogs need to undergo group training to be sure that they can learn and behave around other dogs and people. Starting these dogs off in private training and then transitioning them into group training is a much better solution than just throwing them into a group class in the first week of training.

MY POSITION on veterinary behaviorists is not an overwhelmingly positive one, so I'm not going to expand much on this topic. In general, I would suggest that most of them prescribe far too many medications and use some basic training methods that are not very effective in changing behavior in a significant way. Behaviorists by creed only focus on positive consequences, which greatly limits their training abilities. I hate to be so negative, but I just don't hear good reports often about behaviorists. If you or someone that you know has a different view on this topic, I'm always willing to learn and change my opinion, so please feel free to email me at; ted@tedsbooks.com. One great book by a behaviorist is a book titled *The Dog Who Loved Too Much* by Nicholas Dodman. I highly recommend it.

REAL-WORLD TRAINERS ARE trainers who use a combination of obedience training and state of mind work to produce a dog that is well controlled because of their obedience training, but also in a good state of mind while doing so. It's my view that these are the best option for owners of problematic or dangerous dogs because they focus on what the dogs need to learn, and not a regimented checklist of predetermined tasks. The dogs get obedience training in locations with distraction, which makes them easier to live with and enjoy, but at the same time, the trainers will focus on the dog's state of mind. Over the years, I've seen incredibly well-trained dogs that are not to be trusted, and it's because the trainer never caught the dog's dirty thoughts. This is why real-world training is so effective, it helps dogs make better choices and keeps the dog accountable for bad intentions and actions. A real-world trainer is a good investment if you are struggling with your dog. I would consider myself a real-world trainer because I use a combination of obedience training and behavioral modification when I work with dogs. Also, most real-world trainers will start in private training and progress the dogs into real-world environments as pack walks in urban areas.

WHEN MEETING with any potential trainer or behaviorist, it's important to ask them what they plan to do if the dog does something undesirable. You'll typically get one of two answers;

1. If your dog does something bad, inappropriate, or dangerous, I (the trainer) have completely failed because the dog never should have been put into a situation that pushed them over the edge, resulting in such behavior.
2. We'll have to stop them from acting that way, and then teach them to make better choices.

IF YOU'RE WONDERING, option number two is the better of the two options. A good dog trainer should use some wise judgment when deciding how much distraction is fitting for each dog. They should also know when to go slow and know when to push. Coddling dogs by never allowing them any moments that require conflict resolution is not a great long-term solution if you want your dog to be able to deal with everyday situations.

MANY TRAINERS WILL SUGGEST that teaching a dog a new good habit will allow the dog to forget their old habits, and while that is somewhat true, it's not the entire story. If you really want to have a trustworthy dog, at some point, you will need to use a combination of positive and negative motivations. The negative helps the dog avoid behaviors that we don't want, and the positive will increase the speed and likelihood of seeing behaviors that we want to see. Some trainers teach their clients to avoid so many things that the client and their dog have essentially no life anymore. What good is "training" if you have to run behind your garage the moment you see another dog coming your way? Find a dog trainer that will not avoid conflict over the long term.

# CONTACT AN EXPERIENCED DOG TRAINER

$\mathscr{I}$t can be a challenge to separate the experienced professionals from the amateurs, and this chapter will help you with just that. As a general rule, I don't give actual training advice unless I know a lot about the dog, the people, what they have tried, and what they have not tried. Typically, when you see dog training advice given on the internet, it's very broad, and one size fits all. For example, take the maxim that all dog aggression is based on fear. A preposterous idea that only a brainwashed person with little to no experience could believe, yet people with incorrect thoughts continue to make videos, write blogs, or supply uneducated answers in internet forums. As a general rule, don't take advice from someone unless they know a lot about your dog, and have trained many dogs like yours.

THE DOG TRAINING industry is not a regulated one, and for that reason, you'll find trainers with completely different methodologies and approaches. The world of dog training is made up of everything from terrible trainers to excellent trainers, and plenty in the middle and so this chapter will help you find a dog trainer that will actually help you and not sell you snake oil. The worst thing that a dog trainer can do is to give a dog owner hope without having the experience to back up their claims, and unfortunately, there are a lot of charlatans in the dog training world.

In most industries, you can rely on credentials to help you find a fitting service provider or professional. In the dog training world, many trainers present themselves as qualified trainers by joining professional associations, but these associations are not proof that the trainer is qualified to work with dogs. Most dog training associations don't have in-person requirements to show your skill and ability before joining the association. This means that some can slither under the radar without ever showing their competency. The situation is a weird one because many of the world's most respected dog trainers are not decorated with certificates.

There are really only a hand full of things that you need to look for in a dog trainer if you have a problem dog. They should have years of experience, and they should have experience with the specific issues that your dog has. Remember that experience and time working as a dog trainer are two entirely different things. If you have a German Shepherd with dog aggression issues, I am one of the most experienced trainers in the world because I've rehabilitated about 300 dog aggressive German Shepherds over the years. Technically speaking, I've only been training dogs for ten years, and others have far more time invested as a dog trainer, yet I'm still the professional to seek because of my experience with your dog's breed and issues. They should also be able to show you testimonials from clients they have worked with in the past who owned dogs like yours. If they don't have these things, do not hire them.

Here are a few questions you can ask dog trainers if you have a difficult dog;

- Do you train dogs part-time or full time?

- How many months or years have you been training dogs?
- Did you go to a dog training school, work under a mentor, or are you self-taught?
- Have you ever worked with any dogs like mine before?
- If so, how many, and how are those dogs doing now?
- How long will I need to continue to train my dog once we start?
- Do you have any past clients that I might be able to contact?
- What would the game plan with my dog if we chose you to help us?
- What type of methods and dog training tools would you use if you trained my dog?

CLEARLY, these questions are out of line if you are looking for a basic obedience trainer, but if your dog has severe issues, it's important to know that your trainer is actually going to be able to help you. Unfortunately, it's common for me to have dog owners come in for training who have worked with one or more dog trainers before getting to me, and it's not unusual for me to work with clients who have worked with 2-4 trainers or more.

AS A GENERAL RULE, you'll want to remember that when you are looking for a dog trainer, you are going to invest a lot of time and money if you want to do things the right way. Personally, I know hundreds of incredible dog trainers around the world, and only a hand full of them offer rehabilitation programs under the price of $1000. Don't expect it to be cheap. A good rule to follow is that inexpensive training usually produces lackluster results and short-term results.

SO WHY DOES a good dog training cost so much money? There are a few reasons, but essentially mainly it comes down to the level of support that these trainers give. A good trainer knows that they will have to invest a lot of time into clients with significant issues, and so the price is not cheap. Trainers who work with aggressive dogs who charge hourly rates are to be avoided.

Most good trainers charge per program, not per hour. When I first started to train dogs professionally, I did what many trainers do when they are early in their career, I charged my clients per hour. After only six months, I realized that I had a terrible problem on my hands. Many of my clients would only do a few lessons with me, and then not book any more lessons. This is a problem because the clients would convince themselves that they could take a break from training for a few months and then start again when they had more time or funds. This creates serious issues that produce inconsistency in the home, and often a false sense of security because the client is starting to see some good changes.

Today, I absolutely refuse to work with clients unless they commit to me over the long term, because in the early years, I watched dozens of clients fail miserably over the long term because they got too comfortable in the short term. Frequently, I would get calls from clients after not hearing from them for 3-6 months. Most of these clients stopped after two private lessons because they were either happy with the results, or they needed to save up more money, or they just got complacent.

The trainers that will get you mind-blowing results that last do not want to put their name behind clients who are going to do half of the work. Investing half of the work into a dangerous dog is like doing half of a root canal. If you are not familiar, a root canal is a dental procedure that is done when the root in a person's tooth has died and is rotting inside of the tooth. The pain can be unbearable. When the dentist drills into the tooth, there can be an escape of pressure, and that release will relieve the pressure and pain temporarily, but the process has just started. Next, the dentist will clean out the infection and decay from the inside of the tooth, and then fill the hole to prevent food and other matter from entering the inside of the tooth.

Dog training with a problematic or dangerous dog is like having a root canal. It doesn't end when the pain has decreased, the procedure is done when the dentist has gotten to the root of the issue. Yes, I intended for that pun. Align yourself with a trainer that is not going to leave you in the chair with a hole in your tooth. You might not like the price tag, but it's the only way to go if you have a dangerous or problematic dog.

# I'VE TRIED EVERYTHING!

*I*t's common for dog owners who are struggling to think that they have tried everything. This phrase is one that we dog trainers take with a grain of salt because we know that the owners have not tried everything. I've noticed that more often than not, the owners who claim they have tried everything are the ones who have tried just a handful of things. Clearly, there are struggling dog owners who are really trying and have tried many training styles and many trainers without much success. However, these owners and dogs are in the minority, not the majority.

WHEN A POTENTIAL CLIENT tells me that they have tried everything, I simply ask them why they are calling me if they have tried everything. Silence. Next, I will ask them what things they have tried. In most cases, the dog owners have tried less than 5% of the potential methods or techniques that instantly come to my mind. When many owners think that they have tried everything, it's more common that the owner has convinced themselves that they have done everything when, in reality, they are mistaking the act of struggling with trying different methods.

. . .

SURELY THERE IS a time and a place for starting a specific method and giving it some time to run its course but let me assure you that if your new method, technique, or tool is not working after a few months, you should probably move on and do something that actually moves the needle.

IF YOU FEEL that you have tried everything with your dog, the reality is that you have actually tried everything that you know to try, and likely outsourced other perspectives via the internet, family, friends, TV shows, and dog trainers. These perspectives can actually be extremely damaging if you trust the wrong perspective. I've heard from hundreds of dog owners over the years who had almost completely given up on their dog because their veterinarian had suggested that there was no hope for their dog. When someone such as a veterinarian plants a seed like that in your mind, it's hard to look past their viewpoint because we see veterinarians as professionals who know a lot about dogs. Always seek a 2nd, 3rd, 4th, 5th opinion. Why? Because there is a chance that one of those trainers might not agree with the suggestion to euthanize. And when your dog's heart stops beating, it's game over, no more chances for 2nd opinions.

ALWAYS REMEMBER that there is a way to help the vast majority of dogs. If you call a dog trainer and they are not helpful, call another one. If you've called all of the trainers in your city, call the rest of the trainers in your state. In the chapter that focused on picking a dog trainer, I outlined the importance of not just calling a dog trainer but calling one that actually knows what they are doing. If you call a dog trainer five miles from you because they are the closest trainer to your home, it's extremely unlikely that you are going to connect with a trainer who will know what they are doing. It's not uncommon for people to drive hours to come in for training with me because I am the first and only trainer who actually gave them hope that their dogs were redeemable. If you have a trainer of vet tell you that there is no hope for your dog, it's extremely likely that the person that you are talking to is not the person that you should be talking to. Why allow yourself to be brought down by negative Nancy's who don't know a darn thing about rehabilitating difficult dogs.

I'VE VERY cautious about who I ask advice from because I know how many millions of unqualified people in the world will give advice that they are not qualified to give. Three years ago, I took my dog BB to my vet because he was having a hard time pooping. It was very difficult to watch my dog struggle for over an hour each day, trying to poop without much success. My vet suggested that it could be cancer, drew some blood from the lump on his bum, and sent it away to the laboratory. Three days later, we had good news, but no answers. It was not cancer, but my vet was unable to determine the cause of the issue. She looked at me sadly and told me, "Well, Ted, you'll know when it's time." I was furious. I left and never went back. This vet had been a vet for over 25 years, and she was suggesting that I euthanize a dog that was having a hard time pooping.

AS TIME WENT ON, I found a better solution by going to a local pet store to see if they had any suggestions that might help. The staff member listened to the problem and suggested a dehydrated food called Honest Kitchen. She told me that I could add extra water to the food when hydrating it, and that might help him pass the food more easily. After just a few days, I saw a noticeable change. No answers yet, but this pet store employee had at least given me some advice that had helped alleviate some of my dog's discomfort.

SOME MONTHS LATER, I took BB to another vet for a completely unrelated issue. While I was in the clinic, I asked the vet about the lump on my dog's bum, which I believed was causing his constipation issue and the vet told me in a moment's notice that it was a hernia. "Yeah, they are pretty common. We can do surgery to help, but it's not something that I suggest because the surgery doesn't always work over the long term with older dogs. Just go to your nearest drug store and buy some lactulose to put in his food, which will make it easy for him to poop. He'll be fine." She was correct, and I'm glad to report that BB is pooping regularly without pain over three years later.

SOMETIMES THE PEOPLE that you would expect would know a lot, actually know very little. Sometimes the people that you don't expect to know a lot will surprise you.

WHEN BB WAS SEVEN, he was having some serious pain issues when walking. BB is a very stoic dog, so when he shows that he's in pain, I know that things are beyond painful. I took him to a local vet, and she did some simple testing on him. Range of motion examinations that one would think would cause him pain. She was baffled that she could not notice where his pain was coming from. I left the vet office crushed and without answers. If you've watched your dog cry out in extreme agony, you know the gut-wrenching feeling.

A FEW WEEKS LATER, I was talking to a friend of mine who also has a Belgian Malinois, and she highly recommended that I call the vet that she takes her dog to. "She does chiropractic, laser, and acupuncture. She's unbelievable. I've seen her heal dogs with her hands that every other local vet wanted to operate on." It was clear who I needed to call, so I booked BB in for her next open appointment.

THIS SMALL YET MIGHTY Asian woman was very soft-spoken and unassuming, but it was easy to tell how seriously she took her craft. During the first session with BB, things were rather awkward. She had me bring him into her small consultation room that looked like any other small room in a vet clinic. She started touching his back and his neck without saying a word. After 15 minutes without her saying one word, I had to know what was going on. "Doc, what's going on? What's wrong with BB? Any ideas?" She quickly broke the silence to tell me that everything was wrong with BB's skeletal system. I was taken aback because the last vet couldn't find anything wrong with him, and now this vet couldn't find anything right with him. "His neck is completely all over the place, his pelvis is totally out of alignment, and his back is not in good shape. It's incredible that he can even walk, no wonder he's in so much pain."

FINALLY, an answer. Sometimes just knowing what the issue is can be such a relief. Luckily for me, I was sitting in front of one of Canada's best chiropractic veterinarians. She helped BB in just two sessions at a total cost of $300 plus tax for all of her life-changing services. That $300 was the best money I have ever spent.

IN THE FIRST STORY, I was given better advice for free from a young woman at a pet store than the advice I was given by a veterinarian. That advice was followed up by amazing advice from another vet who instantaneously knew what the problem was and how it could be managed. In the second story, I was given no hope or answers by a qualified vet, only to be given incredible advice and support by another vet. The point that I'm trying to drive home is that we, as dog owners, should not lose hope because one vet or one trainer tells us to give up. There is an incredible trainer or veterinarian out there who is waiting to completely change your life.

I LIKE to work with every dog that comes in for an evaluation so that the clients can see that there is hope. Often, I've had people say that I was able to achieve more with their dog in five minutes than their previous trainer was able to in months of training. Because I only work with difficult and dangerous dogs and I know that people might put their dogs to sleep if you can't get the dog to change in short order, I'm very diligent about not only telling people how I can help, but I also to show them that I can help.

IF YOU THINK that you've tried everything, that's impossible. There are literally thousands of dog training techniques and tools on the market. I always ask dog owners who are struggling with which tools they have used. The vast majority of them have tried a harness, a clicker, and a gentle leader. "Wait a sec, you've tried everything? You haven't even tried 5% of the tools that are available." It's extremely rare that I have clients who have used more offensive looking tools when they come in for training. Tools like a prong collar or electric collar, tools that I use every day to help save dog's lives. If you haven't used any tools that are capable of administering negative motivation, you cannot, for one moment, tell me that you have tried everything.

MUCH OF THE science that dog training was founded on in the 1950-1970s was conducted by a man named B. F. Skinner. His research included both positive and negative consequences. He studied humans, dogs, and other animals, and his results were rather simple. If the consequences that were presented were bad (or negative), there was a high chance that the action would not be repeated. On the flip side, if the consequences were good (or positive), the probability of the action being repeated became stronger.

I DON'T judge dog owners who are skeptical about using these types of tools to train their dogs. No dog owner in their right mind would want to make their dog feel uncomfortable, and that includes me. However, I've always thought that it was interesting how many dog owners can justify paying a veterinarian money to perform a procedure on their dog like a spay or neuter that they know will be uncomfortable. If that is the case, why do so many of them struggle with using corrections to train their dogs? Every year, millions of dogs are spayed or neutered. These dogs don't need to be sexually altered to save their lives, yet millions of these procedures are done on dogs each year without anyone asking the dog if they want to be de-sexed. We knowingly cause dogs pain and discomfort in the case of surgical treatments but refuse it as a way to save a dog's life by way of training.

I BLAME this emotionally charged trend on dog trainers. It's common to hear dog trainers say things like, "If you can't train a dog without discomfort, you shouldn't even be able to call yourself a dog trainer." Would they say that to a vet? These trainers are inadvertently killing dogs when they poison the minds of dog owners with these utopian maxims. Some dog owners believe the lies that are being spouted off by people who don't spend their days working with difficult dogs.

ANOTHER REASON why people avoid using tools like prong collars and electric collars is that many believe that these tools actually make dogs aggressive. Hogwash, I could not disagree more. When you use these tools correctly, they do not make the problem worse, they decrease the likelihood of seeing specific behaviors as mentioned in the B. F. Skinner findings. This lie has been propagated in large part by dog trainers who have told the world that electric collars (also known as e-collars) cause aggression because they cause dogs to fight even harder if used when dogs are in a dog fight.

A FEW YEARS AGO, I had a dog owner call me and ask for help with his dog. He told me that his dog had been e-collar trained, so I asked him which electric collar he had used on his dog, and how he had used it. He told me that his dog was getting into dog fights at the park, so he went to Walmart and bought an e-collar. He then went directly to the dog park, he put the e-collar on his dog and waited until his dog ran up to another dog. He corrected his dog at level 5 out of 10 and was stunned that his dog kept fighting. The dog thought that the e-collar stimulation was coming from the other dog. That doesn't happen when you learn how to properly use the tool and do preliminary training with a professional before using it around other dogs. The fact that a small percentage of people use the tool incorrectly does not mean that the tool is incapable of being effective.

I'VE HELPED save over 1750 dog's lives, and most times, I use tools like e-collars and prong collars. From time to time, I will have people call me and be skeptical about such tools. Of course, I am understanding of their current mental model of these tools, but I can't help but ask them why I'm able to use these tools to save dogs' lives if they think that they make dogs more aggressive.

ANY TOOL CAN BE USED to harm or to help, how that plays out is up to the owner. A knife can be used to help a parent prepare a meal for their family, or that knife could be used to harm their family. A medication correctly prescribed can save a dog's life, a medication incorrectly prescribed can lead to a dog's sudden death. What is meant for good, can be misused, regardless of the tool that is used?

USING corrective collars is not an instant fix, it's a faster fix. When you are struggling with your dog, speed is important despite what many dog trainers will tell you. They will tell you that your dog's happiness is the most important thing. What they don't often tell you is that positive-only training takes more time and skill to implement with dangerous dogs, and that additional time kills millions of dogs each year. Find someone who can help you decide which tools might be a good option for you and your dog. Read books on the topic. Learn from online courses, do whatever you have to do to save your dog's life.

IT'S SIMPLE MATH; if you believe that you tried everything, you haven't. I've been training dogs six days a week for 10 years, and I still haven't tried everything.

. . .

FOR MOST DOGS, prong collars can instantly stop a dog from pulling about 70% of the time. This 70% change in behavior is due to the tool and not the technique. Problems can arise when clients buy a prong collar and don't properly fit the collar. Prong collars are designed to be tightly fitted on your dog's neck, and they become rather ineffective when they have too many links installed. Another thing that I see from time to time is dog owners who buy plastic prong collars. These collars look less offensive, but rarely prove to be effective. Plastic prong collars are a waste of time and money, in my opinion, because many dogs still pull on the leash, which is problematic because then the owners think that the metal prong collars will not work either.

IF YOU'RE STRUGGLING with your dog pulling on the leash or reacting towards people or dogs, another good tool for leash walking is called the transitional leash. It's similar to a head halter, but it makes it much more difficult for the dogs to get off their heads. You don't need to be very strong to control a small-large sized dog with one of these collar/leash combos. You can buy them at www.k9lifeline.net.

IF YOU DON'T plan to train your dog, and just want to buy a collar for your dog that they will not be able to get out of, the martingale collar is about the best that I have used. When I have a Houdini dog, there is a martingale collar on the dog at every moment. They are very ineffective for correcting pulling and other bad behaviors, but they are an insurance policy if your dog tries to back out of collars or harnesses. Many people use a martingale collar and a prong collar at the same time attached to one leash, in case one of the collars wear to break or come apart.

E-COLLARS (ELECTRIC COLLARS) can be an incredible advantage for a myriad of reasons. On-leash, off-leash, behavioral problems, while a dog is swimming, the list goes on. There is, however, a greater learning curve to using e-collars over most other dog training tools. E-collars require more training on the part of the owner in order to do things correctly. When I say much more, it's really only about four weeks, but it's not the kind of tool that you will want to put on your dog and just start pressing buttons. You're right to be cautious about using these tools, but you also need to be realistic. If you are thinking about putting your dog down, whatever you do in an effort to save their life is of benefit, even if you don't do it perfectly. Keep an open mind when thinking about tools and techniques. Use plenty of positive things in your training like praise, food, treats, toys to let your dog know that they have done a good job, but you should also have the right tools on hand to correct your dog's bad behaviors.

IF YOU ARE interested in these tools, I have dedicated books on these topics and online courses on my website; www.tedsbooks.com.

# MY DOG HAS NO TRIGGER

*I*t's common that dog owners will tell me that their dog has no trigger. "It comes out of nowhere" is often something that I hear as owners are seeking help. Unless your dog has a very rare form of neurologically-based aggression, which I discussed in a previous chapter, your dog has a trigger or multiple triggers, and you are just missing it. I'm not at all, suggesting that you should be able to notice your triggers. You are not a professional, in fact, you are a different species, this is why learning how to read your dog's vocal communication and body language will be a challenge for most dog owners.

WHEN I MEET with clients for the first time and start asking questions, with about 95% accuracy, I can figure out the trigger within 15-20 minutes of watching the dog and by talking to the owners. Every day I meet with people who have leash reactive or aggressive dogs; most of those owners report little to no change in behavior before their dog freaks out at another dog. The most frequent change in behavior that is noted is that some owners notice that their dog's hair stands upon his/her back.

. . .

MY FIRST STEP is to walk them through the five steps of leash reactivity. In these steps, we see a step by step breakdown each dog will progress through before a leash explosion.

STEP ONE IS SCANNING; scanning from side to side. Usually, it starts the moment the dog walks outside the front door of the owner's home. It's hunting really, but rarely noticed by dog owners.

STEP TWO IS ears locked forward. Some owners spot this, but only about 10%. Ears forward when a leash reactive dog is focusing on another dog is not a good sign. It's a sign of fixation.

STEP THREE IS SEEN in the dog's tail. Up high in the air, it's telling the world that the dog is overstimulated and about to make a bad choice. The closer the tail transitions towards the dogs back, the more fixated the dogs are. A high tail that is bouncy is often seen as a happy tail, and surely it can be, but with a leash reactive dog, it's not something that I want to see. A high stiff tail is even worse as it's indicative of a dog's desire for aggression.

STEP FOUR IS HEARD NOT SEEN. Escalated breathing, or as I refer to it, loaded breathing is something that happens when a dog is close to an explosion. The dog is taking in additional oxygen to prepare for the soon to come explosion.

LASTLY, on some dogs, we will notice that their hair stands upon their backs. For some, it's just a patch of hair over the shoulders. For others, it's over the shoulders, and over the hips at the base of the tail, and for others still, it's all the way from the shoulders to the tip of the tail.

. . .

IN MY ESTIMATION, most dog owners miss the majority of what their dog is speaking through their body language and vocalizations. It's interesting how most dog owners know 30 seconds before their dog poops by the subtle changes in the way that they walk, however, miss mountains of information that is pointing to changes in behavior that are leading to them freaking out at other dogs, people, cars, animals, etc.

THE WIDER ISSUE here is that when we miss our dogs' nasty state of mind. We let them think dirty thoughts and get away with them. Every time your dog freaks out at another dog, they are intimidating the other dog to stay out of their space. That's not good. When we let our dogs walk around the neighborhood like a psychopath with a hunting rifle, that's not good. When we let our dogs lose their minds every time a person walks by your home, do you think that that is going to have positive implications or negative ones when the UPS driver comes to drop off a package? When your dog is guarding everything in sight 24 hours a day, it becomes very easy for them to over-generalize. That short fuse now seems like it doesn't even exist anymore because your dog is always ready to snap.

IF YOU ARE CONVINCED that your dog has a short fuse, you'll need to get good at two things. First, you'll want to get better at reading your dog's body language and vocalizations, then learn how to limit their explosions so that the habit can be broken. If going for a walk with your dog is like watching someone try and walk a velociraptor, have a friend go out with you on a walk and videotape you walking your dog from the other side of the street. It will be embarrassing, so drive out to another neighborhood where no one knows you so that you look incompetent around people that you don't know. Have your friend video the entire 10-15 minutes' walk. Your dog walking out of the home, down the front steps, up to your driveway, getting into your car, getting out of the car, walking down the street, past a few dogs and people. When you return home, review the video footage. You'll find great value in watching your dog from another angle, but don't just fast forward to the part where your dog freaks out at another dog. Write down notes as you watch the video taking time to note your dog's scanning, ear position, tail position, etc. Learn anything interesting? Were you missing anything that you can now see? I bet you see your leash walks in a very different light.

RIGHT NOW, invest 15 minutes of your time by getting a piece of paper and a pen and writing down some simple questions.

- What are the things that trigger your dog?
- When is your dog triggered?

IF YOU KNOW what triggers your dog, you can safely take precautions so that your dog is not a danger to other people, dogs, or animals. Directly after something happens, write down notes that will help you better control your dog in the future. If you go for a walk and your dog barks at every other dog, then note that. Also, note that you walked by three other dogs. One was a Husky, one a Golden, and one a small white dog. Do you know anything about these dogs? Do you know if any of them are male or female? If you hear their owner calling telling Roxy to stop pulling on the leash, you can assume that they own a female dog.

DOGS CAN BE TRIGGERED by hundreds of different things. In an effort to help you brainstorm ideas for your dog, let's look at a few of the most common triggers.

Dog/Dog Issues;

- Size of the other dog
- Color of the other dog

- The energy of the other dog
- Past history with the other dog
- Competition over resources
- How many seconds was there between when your dog noticed the other dog and when they reacted inappropriately?
- Is your dog more defensive at home, in your yard, or on walks?
- Is your dog more defensive in the morning, afternoon, or after the sun goes down?
- Does your dog guard people or resources when other dogs are around?

Dog/Human Issues:

- Height of the person
- Age of the person
- Sex of the person
- Color of the person's skin
- Did the person give the dog even brief or consistent eye-contact?
- Did the person move quickly?
- Was the person intoxicated?
- Where was the dog when they reacted aggressively?
- Did the person do anything of note before the dog reacted to them?
- Was the dog reminded of another person with a similar look or temperament?
- Is your dog more defensive at home, in your yard, or on walks?
- Is your dog more defensive in the morning, afternoon, or after the sun goes down?

# AGGRESSION, REACTIVITY, CONTROLLING AND TREADMILL DOGS

*R*eactivity is a behavior that is seen and heard; barking, growling, lunging. Aggression also has many of these same symptoms. However, aggression is about intention. Simply put, a reactive dog makes a lot of noise and looks very aggressive when in reality these dogs are all bark and little to no bite. I work with roughly 40-50 dogs each year that go to doggy daycare five days a week. These dogs are insane on the leash when we start, and their behavior to the untrained eye looks like aggression. I know that most of these dogs are just frustrated because they want to go and say hello to another dog.

SOME DOGS FIND themselves in dog fights without attempting to start a fight. I call these dogs treadmill dogs. These dogs tend to be extremely high energy dogs that rush into social situations without taking stock of the situation. These dogs are extremely social, but they lack impulse control. They often look at other dogs like a treadmill instead of a play partner, something to release energy rather than a partner. The idea of a partner denotes give and take, respect, and regulation of emotions. These dogs lack impulse control, emotional control, and respect. They use other dogs to get what they want. These dogs run over to other dogs as fast as they possibly can and into another dog's personal space. It can be very irritating for some dogs when they are approached in this way, which often results in one dog growling in an effort to get the other dog to back off and give them some space. The dog that rushes over then reacts to this growl, by starting a scrap or fight. It's a vicious cycle.

THIS WHOLE PROBLEM could have been avoided if the overstimulated dog had some impulse control and showed some respect to the other dog. These dogs are often seen as being social dogs because they can get along with other dogs that also act in the same way. However, they tend to butt heads with other dogs that are calm and respectful. More often than not, when these dogs are involved in a fight, it's actually an argument. Surely they find themselves in scraps from time to time, but they avoid serious fights that result in physical damage. These scraps to the untrained eye look terrible, and they are very vocal. Frequently the dogs go up on their hind legs, mouths open, growling. Humans commonly overreact to these arguments by yelling, and putting their hands in the blur of dog teeth and pissed off dog owners. In most cases, these dogs will argue for 10-15 seconds and then walk away from each other with an understanding and an absence of blood and wounds needing to be sewn up.

AN AGGRESSIVE DOG tends to be more quiet and unassuming. These dogs mentally think about what they are doing before they do it, while reactive dogs are more driven by frustration. Aggressive dogs can develop hatred towards other dogs or other people. They can be driven by predatory impulses, territorial triggers, resource competition, or grudges. You'll know if your dog is aggressive if they attack other dogs/humans and seriously hurt them even if they have five seconds or less to be damage. They are calculated and can injure or kill in seconds.

. . .

SOME DOGS SEEK control over other dogs. If your dog is a controlling dog, you'll notice that they are calm in nature, and they pin other dogs on the ground without hurting them. I've met hundreds of large dogs over the years that were incorrectly diagnosed by other dog trainers as being dog aggressive when they were actually dogs that struggled with control issues. Many of these dogs would even pick up small dogs in their mouth and hold them until they calmed down, or pinned them on the ground. Of course, the small dogs act dramatically by screaming like they are dying. However, when examined, the small dogs are without physical injury. This begs the question. Was the desire of the controlling dog to harm the other dog, or was it to contain them in an effort to regulate their energy? Calm dogs that pin other dogs are not aggressive, they are like security guards.

THE ROLE of a security guard is not to prosecute a theft or a belligerent drunk. Their role exists to contain the problem until the proper authorities can be notified. Pinning another dog serves several purposes in the dog world. In the animal world, it's most often used to regulate a dog's toxic energy when they are not self-regulating. Pinning is also helpful to show other members of the pack what energies are ok and not ok. It's all about energy control.

- Reactive dogs are all bark and no bite and rarely cause injuries
- Aggressive dogs desire to hurt other dogs and often cause injuries
- Controlling dogs desire to contain and control other dogs with toxic energy and rarely cause injuries
- Treadmill dogs are social in nature, annoying to be around and rarely cause injuries

IT's important to know the intention of your dog so that you can better define how dangerous they actually are.

# DOG TRAINING OR CONTAINMENT?

*W*hen dog owners have a dangerous dog who's bitten people or dogs, the first thing that needs to be discussed is how the owners are going to prevent these things from happening in the future. The restrictions that I suggest for clients who are at the beginning of training can, at times, ruffle feathers. Dog training with dangerous dogs has to require safety precautions, that's a given. The trainer needs to feel safe, the owner should feel safe, other humans, dogs, and animals in the dog owner's neighborhood should also feel safe and be safe.

IN CHAPTER FOUR, I mentioned that I have aggressive dogs on my property every day and never have to break up dog fights or take people to the hospital for stitches. When I wrote that chapter several months ago, I did not do a complete job of illustrating why it's so easy for me to avoid these issues, and why it's so hard for dog owners to avoid these issues in their homes. The first reason why dog owners give their dogs so much freedom is that dog owners love their dogs as much as they love many humans in their lives, and that causes them to feel badly when they have to restrict their dog's freedom in any way.

The second reason that restricting freedom is so hard for dog owners is because dogs are well equipped to manipulate their humans, which can cause the owners to cave and allow their dog unearned freedom.

I SEE this in my own life when I'm spending time with my 4-year-old daughter. She asks to watch a cartoon, and I tell her no. She asks again, hugging me. "Just for a few minutes, I promise. Please daddy," she asks me as she tries her best to look cute and innocent. Dogs do these kinds of things every day, the difference is simply that this manipulation can cost a dog their life if the human caves.

"HE WHINES INCESSANTLY when we go for a walk as we walk past the local park, and I just feel so bad that I can't let him off leash to run around" is something that many dog owners have said who regretted letting their dog off-leash when they were not capable of such freedom. Dogs get killed by cars every day who are owned by people who would swear that their dogs come when called 90% of the time. As well, dogs are euthanized every day because people allowed their dog the option to run to the front door, bark, and bite the person at the front door.

DOG TRAINING IS a lot of work and costs a lot of money to do correctly, but containing a dangerous dog does not cost much money. While containment can be achieved instantly, many dog owners struggle with the thought of restricting their dog's freedom because it touches something deep inside of people. Humans have a strong urge to give their dogs what they want, even if it's dangerous for others. In short, saying no is far more difficult than saying yes.

IN KEEPING your dog from doing something dangerous, I've included a list of dog training tools you'll want to purchase to help keep everyone safe in the coming weeks, months, and years. More on these safety measures in the coming chapters.

- *Dog Crates* - Helpful for clients who need to contain their dogs for the safety of others
- *Muzzles* - Important for dog owners whose dogs act aggressively towards them
- *Martingale Collars* - Helpful for clients who own dogs who know how to back out of collars and harnesses
- *Baby Gates* - Helpful for clients who need to contain their dogs inside the home. Best used to deter dogs from running out of the house when a door is left open
- *E-collar* - Helpful for clients who own dogs who don't have a reliable recall
- *Prong Collar* - Helpful for clients who own dogs who pull on the leash and can drag their owns with them
- *Transitional Leash* - A leash and collar combination that is helpful for clients who own dogs who pull on the leash

IF YOU OWN A DANGEROUS DOG, your most urgent task is not to train them, but to contain them. Your primary concern should be to keep them from doing anything dangerous. Purchase baby gates, get a dog crate, buy a muzzle, get the correct leashes and collars as soon as you possibly can. When your dog is acting aggressively with strangers, containment is simple. Lock your doors, set up baby gates, muzzle your dog when outside, and you don't have a problem.

WHEN DOGS ARE dangerous to those that they live with, things get very complicated. Your safety is in jeopardy. Don't do anything that could make your dog try and bite you. If you own multiple dogs that are fighting, keep them separated 100% of the day until you can get some help. Your dog's feelings should not be taken into account in these times. Choose your safety and the safety of others over your dog's feelings. You can decide what to do next only after making your home safe. It will take you some time to decide how to progress with your dog, Training, rehoming, euthanizing, these options require some time to decide and need to come after you are able to create a safe home free of dangerous behavior.

# WRITE A LETTER TO YOUR DOG'S NEW OWNERS

*I*f you ultimately decide to rehome your dog, one of the most loving things that you can do for your dog is to take an hour to write down a detailed history of your dog's life so that a potential adopter will have as much information about your dog as possible. This exercise will help your dog immensely if they are adopted into a new home. Write your dog's history, likes, dislikes, what happened to him, and what you know didn't happen to him. When the new owner is armed with this important knowledge, it will be much easier for your dog to settle into a new home. Be specific. If your dog is afraid of swimming, be honest about why your dog is afraid of swimming. If they were forced into the water at a young age and have avoided the water since that time, include that in your letter. If they are like many dogs that don't like water and didn't have anything bad happen to them, include that in the letter too. If you know that your dog is afraid of men, document that in the letter and remember to include information about why you think they are afraid of men.

TELLING the new owners what did happen to your dog is very important, but in some ways, it's more important for them to know what didn't happen to your dog. As a dog trainer, I meet incredible people every day who have adopted dogs with issues. These issues are often made much worse by the new owners not having a history of their new dog. Personally, I've seen dozens of dog owners who were convinced that their dog was physically beaten because they noticed their new dog ran out of the kitchen when the broom fell on the ground. If your dog has had an unnoteworthy upbringing, write these things down in your letter. If your dog is shy with new people, document the situation accurately. "He's never been beaten, he's never been hit. He's shy of new people because we didn't properly socialize him as a puppy, and he's always been timid. He warms up to people quickly if they give him a treat and ignore him for a few moments and avoid eye contact."

IT WILL BE easy for the new owners of your dog to create a myth about what they think its past life was like, and this myth will not be accurate and possibly harmful. If you don't let people know that he was not abused, they might assume that he was, which typically ends up culminating in excessive codling. It's easy for us humans to create these myths and stories to give ourselves answers, but rarely do these tales ever amount to anything positive or helpful. Excuses are often formed as a result of these created myths as a way for us humans to feel compassion for the new dog. Surely compassion is a great superpower for a dog owner to have, but excuses are not a good indication of compassion.

PEOPLE WILL MAKE assumptions if you don't tell them what they should expect. I've encountered hundreds of new dog owners who were convinced that their new dog was neglected in their previous home simply because their dog doesn't like to play tug of war or play fetch. Some dogs just don't like playing fetch, and you'll want to tell people that in your letter.

. . .

I'VE SEEN dog owners decide not to crate train their dog because they were convinced that their dog was left in a crate for 18 hours a day without any evidence to promote this idea. So, where did this myth come from? It was conceived in the mind of the new dog owner because they brought home a crate and their new rescue dog didn't want to go into the crate. The dog whined for five minutes before the new owners felt bad for her and let her out. This myth, of course, resulted in the dog destroying the new owner's home, which resulted in the dog going back to the shelter. A perfectly good dog missed out on a perfectly good home because her previous owner didn't invest the time to tell her new owners what to expect.

LET'S look at some of the things you'll want to mention in your letter;

- ANY POTENTIAL BITE history your dog might have with people
  - Specific people your dog might be wary of
  - Specific triggers that you might have noticed when your dog is around people
  - How is your dog around cats?
  - How is your dog around children?
  - Specific dogs that your dog might be wary of
  - Does your dog like to swim?
  - Is your dog afraid of thunderstorms?
  - Is your dog afraid of fireworks?
  - How does your dog react when you leave them alone?
  - Does your dog enjoy playing fetch or tug?
  - What type of toys does your dog like?
  - What are your dog's favorite treats?
  - What kind of food did were you feeding your dog?
  - Is your dog crate trained?
  - Is your dog picky with their food?
  - What are things that stress your dog out?

• How does your dog react in the car? On short drives and on long drives
• How does your dog act when they go to the veterinarian

# SURRENDERING TO AN ANIMAL SHELTER

*a* dog being in a shelter is never ideal. Dogs can deteriorate very quickly in an animal shelter despite the love that is typically bestowed upon the dogs by the shelter staff and volunteers. Statistically speaking, most dogs are surrendered because of behavioral problems, and in many cases, these are common issues like jumping up on people, running out of the front door, pulling on the leash, and excessive barking. All of these issues are relatively easy to solve with a proper dog training program.

IF YOU ARE THINKING about surrendering your dog to a shelter, there are a few things to consider before doing that.

## HUMAN AGGRESSIVE DOGS GOING TO SHELTERS

In many places around North America, dogs that have a bite history with people typically are euthanized within 24-48 hours of being surrendered to the shelter. Most shelters are overflowing with dogs that need homes, and housing a dog with a known bite history is a liability for the staff working in the shelter. I'm not at all suggesting that these dogs should not have access to a loving home or space in a shelter; I'm just letting you in on the way that most shelters think. Most shelters are staffed in large part by volunteers, and in many cases, they have limited knowledge to aid them when keeping themselves safe around human aggressive dogs. In addition to that fact, the shelter has to take into account the safety of the adopters and the people and animals that would be living near to the dog if they are rehomed.


### DOG AGGRESSIVE DOGS GOING TO SHELTERS

The moment that you surrender your dog to a shelter, you lose ownership over your dog, and you lose the ability to suggest who should be able to adopt your dog. Apart from losing their dog, this is the hardest thing for dog owners to grapple with when surrendering their dog; the inability to have to say into the dog's future. Questions will buzz around in your head like the relentless thoughts that a parent ponders over the first time their child goes away to sleep away camp. "Will Rover ever forgive me? Will Rover find a home or be put down? Will Rover always remember me, or will he forget about me quickly? How long will Rover be in the shelter before Rover finds a home?" These questions haunt many dog owners, and unlike a parent whose child is at sleep-away camp, your dog is not coming back in seven days and six nights.


YOU MIGHT ALSO FIND yourself second-guessing your decision as more questions start to flood into your brain. "Could I have done something sooner so that things didn't have to come to this? Did I let Rover down? We didn't get a dog so that we could give up on them, how could I have failed him so? Was there something wrong with Rover from the start? Did I do everything that I could have been done?"


FORTUNATELY, animal shelters are more sympathetic to dogs with dog aggression issues, as opposed to those dogs with human aggression issues. Dog aggression cases don't carry the same level of liability, and these dogs are easier for shelter staff to handle. These dogs often find loving homes in homes that don't have another dog living in them.

## DOGS WITH BEHAVIORAL ISSUES GOING TO SHELTERS

If you ask animal shelter workers why most dogs are surrendered to the shelter, the answer that you will hear most often is going to be because of behavioral problems. Excessive barking, getting out of the yard, jumping up on people, pulling on the leash, stealing food from the counter are all issues that unfortunately have landed millions of dogs in animal shelters over the years. Many of these dogs are really nice dogs that can easily be trained to stop doing these behaviors, but for a myriad of reasons, people give up on these dogs.

IF YOU ARE CONSIDERING SURRENDERING your dog because of simple issues like these I'm going to suggest that you reconsider. Surely if you are reading this book I can assume that you love your dog and want to find a way to keep them. Sometimes it's just one issue that leads owners to surrender their dog, but more frequently there are a handful of behavioral problems that are making a life for the humans so frustrating that it results in the humans surrendering their dog to a shelter. I don't know the shelter system where you live, but things are not pretty in most places around North America. Yes, the staff does the best with what they have, but many shelters euthanize perfectly healthy dogs because they have such a significant amount of dogs coming in each day. Before surrendering your dog, I'm going to suggest a few things.

1. Read this book in its entirety.
2. Call a dog trainer and ask them to help you
3. If you can't find a local dog trainer to help you, shoot me an email and ask for some advice (ted@tedsbooks.com)
4. If you don't have enough money to train your dog the right

way, maybe I can offer some suggestions to get quick results via email. (ted@tedsbooks.com)

# SURRENDERING TO A DOG RESCUE

*O*ver the years, I've had the privilege of helping several local dog rescue organizations. The importance of these organizations in our society cannot be understated. My deep respect for people who work in rescue has been realized because I've watched hard-working people invest their own money in an effort to help the dogs that they care for. It's a thankless job for those who work in the rescue world. These people love these dogs so much that they will endure endless frustrations from humans so that they can help dogs in need.

I'VE BEEN in the room with rescue workers while they've taken phone calls from dog owners who just don't make things easy. A 6-year-old dog that's never been neutered hasn't been to the vet since he was a puppy is looking to be rehomed at a moment's notice because the dog bit the mailman again today. If you want to get a sense of the level of tension in the room when that phone call is received, imagine the level of tension that might be present in the room when a spouse tells their wife or husband that they have been cheating on them for five years. These rescue workers live in constant damage control mode, so please consider their state of mind if you decide to surrender your dog to a rescue organization.

MAKE things as easy as they can be. If at all possible, don't wait until the last possible moment to call them and for goodness sake, do not make demands of them. I've personally had people call me on the phone and be completely shocked that I didn't want to adopt their aggressive dog. "What do you mean you don't want her? You're a dog trainer, right? And you work with aggressive dogs don't you, why won't you take my dog?" I've devoted my life to helping people with their dogs, but why would I want to take in your aggressive dog at a moment's notice when I have not even met your dog?

DON'T MAKE demands of the rescue, and you better avoid playing the guilt card. If a rescue tells you that they can't take your dog for 3-4 weeks because they don't have any fosters who can the animal, don't threaten to put your dog to sleep. That's a low blow, and it will likely cause the conversation to end with a dial tone. Take your dog in for its vaccinations at the vet and get your dog's medical records printed out so that you can give the rescue a copy. Have your dog microchipped while they are at the vet, and have them spayed or neutered if they are not already altered. These are all things that the organization will take into accoun when considering if they will take your dog or not. These vet services cost the rescue organization money, so at least do your part and see that your dog is medically sound. If you don't have the money to spay or neuter your dog, call around your town to see if there is a free spay or neuter clinic that can do the procedure for free or at a reduced price.

## HUMAN AGGRESSIVE DOGS GOING TO A RESCUE

Dogs with a history of human aggression are rarely taken into dog rescue, and the main reason is simple. It's dangerous. While dogs with bite histories are typically turned away, many small dogs seem to avoid these organization-wide regulations because they can't do as much damage to a potential adopter. It's a lot of legal liability, and it's dangerous to take in a medium to a large-sized dog with such issues. Add to that the fees that the rescue will likely have to raise from donors to pay for the dog's training. For a few years, I used to work with these cases for a local rescue before I decided that I needed to stop. Dog/dog aggression sign me up. Rehoming a human aggressive dog...an insane amount of work and liability.

A DOG that is good with their owner is much easier to rehome than a dog that has a history of biting its owner. If your dog has a history of biting you, it's highly unlikely that any dog rescue or shelter will be willing to take your dog and try to find them a new home because it's very likely that your dog will bite the rescue foster or a potential adopter. If your dog has a history of biting strangers, your options will be greater but still less than double-digit figures.

OWNERS of purebred dogs tend to have an easier time finding a home for dogs with human aggression histories if they contact breed-specific rescues. For example, a few years ago, I got a call from a local rescue that I used to help out, and they wanted me to temperament test two dogs that they were thinking of helping. The dogs were living in the same home, and both had a lot of issues including some dog aggression issues. The dogs were both Rhodesian Ridgebacks; so naturally, I looked online and found a local Rhodesian specific rescue. The rescue was based in the USA, but they did have a local contact that I was able to contact about the dogs. Within 24 hours the dogs had been picked up and went to a foster for the organization. Breed fanciers will sometimes go to great lengths to help a dog that is of a breed that they love, despite never meeting the dog.

## DOG AGGRESSIVE DOGS GOING TO A RESCUE
Rehoming dog/dog aggressive dogs is really where dog rescues do

some of their best work. A quick online search will uncover a significant amount of dogs that are "dog selective" or not to be adopted to homes with dogs. A lack of social skills around other dogs is not typically a deal-breaker for most rescues. However, it can make things more challenging for your dog to be placed in a new home because most rescues house their adoptable dogs with fosters. The majority of fosters already have one or more dogs, so it can be a challenge for new selectively social dogs to find a foster home, and many have to wait until a dog-free space opens up.

REHOMING A DOG/DOG aggressive dog is not without potential liability, but many dog rescues incur the potential liability because it's relatively easy to find a loving home for these dogs in homes that don't have another dog. First-time dog owners often adopt these dogs. The rescue will often impose a mandatory rule that the potential adopter must purchase a dog training package before they adopt their new dog as a way to ensure that the new owners will receive some good advice and dog training instruction.

IF YOU'RE CONSIDERING SURRENDERING your dog aggressive dog to a rescue organization, might I suggest that you reconsider? Unless you have multiple dogs in your own home and are frequently dealing with serious dog fights, you can keep your dog safe and away from other dogs. If you surrender your dog aggressive dog, there is a chance that they will be euthanized. Surely, their chances of finding a home are higher than a human aggressive dog, but there's still a possibility that your dog will be put to sleep if the rescue has a hard time placing your dog. If they are able to find a home, which many do, the vast majority of those dogs live somewhat isolated lives with their new owners anyways. Very few dog owners are willing to invest thousands of dollars and months or years of hard work to help a dog repair its lack of social skills around other dogs, and so most of these dogs live somewhat reclusive lives. Some are lucky to be adopted into a home with a fenced-in yard, which opens up some off-leash opportunities but must live a life that revolves around 1-2 leashed walks around the block each day.

I'M NOT at all suggesting that a dog that goes out for 1-2 leashed walks a day is living a terrible life, but I am trying to get at a bigger question, which is; If the worst-case scenario is that your dog is put to sleep for their lack of social skills, and the best-case scenario is that they most likely will live a somewhat reclusive life, why bother rehoming your dog in the first place? A life with you that is restricted to on-leash walks if fine, most dogs live that way in North America. If you had the financial means you could even find a trainer to help you open up a lot of freedom to your dog if they receive the right training.

ALLOW me to outline a few things that you can do to prevent your dog from attacking another dog.

- Set up baby gates before each of your doors that lead outside
- Lock your doors to prevent friends and family from coming into your home and leaving the door open
- Don't have other dogs come over to your home
- If you live in a neighborhood where dogs come out onto the street to bark at you as you walk your dog, you can muzzle your dog, but also you should buy a loud boat horn that you can carry with you to scare off other dogs
- Check your leashes and collars daily for cracks in the metal clasps and tears in the fabric or leather
- Have your dog wear a martingale collar (available on Amazon and any pet store)
- Don't let your dog off-leash unless you are alone and in a fenced area

# REHOMING YOUR DOG

*REHOMING A HUMAN AGGRESSIVE DOG*
Rehoming a human aggressive dog presents many challenges. Finding the right home can take months or years because few people are interested in adopting a human aggressive dog when there are likely hundreds or thousands of dogs in your area that are not human aggressive. I know how harsh these words might sound, but it is a reality when someone is searching the internet to adopt a dog.

Human aggressive dogs can be split into three categories, and they are;

- Dogs that are aggressive to strangers
- Dogs that are aggressive to their owners
- Dogs that are aggressive to strangers and their owners

DOGS THAT ARE aggressive towards strangers and are not aggressive towards their owners obtain the highest likelihood of finding a new home that will adopt them because some dog owners actually want a dog that is protective of them. I've met many women (and some men too) over the years who want their dog to be protective of their home because they are single and live alone. To one man, a sin, to another a blessing. Things get complicated when the dogs are aggressive towards their owners because the new owner is going to be at a large risk of being bitten.

WHATEVER YOU DECIDE, you need to fully communicate your dog's history with any potential adopters. Anything that you leave out about your dog's history that you know about could be used against you if something were to happen, and the new owner was to take you to court and seek damages. Write everything down and have two copies to sign when your dog is being adopted, one copy you will keep, and one copy will go with the new owner. I would highly suggest that you spend some money to consult with a lawyer before rehoming your human aggressive dog; they can give you legal guidance and can help you write up such a document to have the new owner sign.

IT'S ALSO WISE to take your dog to a vet before rehoming your dog so that the new owner will be aware of your dog's health history and current health. Be sure to provide a potential adopter with medical records from your veterinarian. If your dog is given a clean bill of health, your dog will have a higher likelihood of being adopted, and the new adopter will not be able to suggest in the future that you rehomed a sick dog.

IF YOU'VE FOUND someone who wants to adopt your dog, you'll need to do some research on the adopters before sending your dog with a new owner. Whenever possible, it's preferable to rehome to a person that you know or something that you might know of through a friend. Blindly giving your dog to someone that you don't know is not a good idea and it could cause your dog to be given to someone with malicious intentions. If the potential adopter has owned a dog before, ask them if you can call their veterinarian's office to ensure that they will be a good fit. If they have never owned a dog before, it's not likely to be a person that you should be considering because they should have at least a novice understanding of dog behavior if they are adopting a dog with a bite history.

## DOG AGGRESSIVE DOGS BEING REHOMED

Millions of dog aggressive dogs in North America are rehomed each year, some successfully and others less successfully. Often times, these dogs are adopted because it's cheaper to get a free dog than pay a dog rescue or shelter an adoption fee. Adoption fees can vary depending on your location, but as a rule, dogs with issues are given away and not sold. Sometimes these dogs are given to amazing people with great intentions, and other times they are given to people who are less than diligent about keeping them properly contained.

IF YOU ARE GOING to rehome your dog aggressive dog, please do your research on any potential adopters before rehoming your dog. Go to their home and see where your dog will be living. Ensure that they have money to buy food and provide veterinary care. Do your best to ensure that they are not going to be lackadaisical about containing their new dog. Also, ensure that you spay or neuter your dog before rehoming them so that they can't be used in a puppy mill. This will also eliminate any probability that your dog will become pregnant or impregnate another person's dog if the new owner proves not to be diligent about containing their new dog.

# WHEN TO EUTHANIZE YOUR DOG

*W*ords cannot express the pain that humans feel, before, during, and after having to put their best friend to sleep. We, humans, develop deep bonds with our dogs and these bonds can feel as real as the love that a mother would have for her firstborn child. Dogs do many things for us, which is why they are so hard to let go of. Saying goodbye to your best friend because they are old or sick is hard to endure, but saying goodbye to a healthy dog because of their behavior is not something that we can easily wrap our hearts or minds around either.

I HOPE that this book has been non-judgemental up to this point because I don't see how condemnation is of any benefit when someone is considering rehoming their dog or potentially euthanizing them. If you are thinking about either of these things, chances are that you already feel terrible that you've even found yourself in this position. Unfortunately, love doesn't actually fix everything. Some dogs are incredibly difficult to live with and will require a massive amount of work and dedication to aid them in just getting to a normal state.

. . .

THIS BOOK DOES NOT TELL you to rehome your dog, nor will it tell you to train your dog, and it certainly won't tell you when to take your dog to the vet to have them put to sleep. It's not in my nature to tell people what to do, rather I prefer to lay out all of the facts and options and let the person decide what they want to do, and typically I applaud them for whatever choice they make. I see little value in dumping hot coals on the heads of dog owners who are trying their best with what they know.

## WHEN SHOULD YOU CONSIDER EUTHANIZING YOUR DOG?

There are a few situations in which euthanizing a healthy dog should be discussed. When things get so dangerous for the dog owner that they are in constant fear of their own safety, it's time to sit down with your family and veterinarian to talk about the next steps forward. If your dog has one or both of the issues below, euthanizing your dog is something to consider in order to keep yourself and your family safe.

1. When a dog is attacking their own family members and everyone is in danger
2. When a dog has unprovoked aggression that has absolutely no trigger

WHEN A DOG IS ATTACKING their own family, they either need to see a very qualified trainer who works with dogs like this every day or they need to consider putting the dog to sleep. It's hardly responsible for someone to rehome such a dog if we can expect with a high degree of certainty that the dog will also attack their new owner. I work with dogs that have extensive histories of biting their owners, and these dogs can be made to be safe to live with, but that requires that you have an expert dog trainer who can help you locally and it will also require thousands of dollars if you want to do the job correctly.

IF YOU'VE HAD at least one or more professional dog trainers who specialize in working with aggressive dogs tell you that your dog has an untreatable case of neurological aggression that cannot be fixed, the first thing that you should do is have the dog tested for a brain tumor. If the tests come back positive, your dog will likely due to the brain tumor is a short amount of time. If your dog has a brain tumor and it's randomly attacking people, dogs, animals, or both due to the tumor, you should talk with your family and veterinarian to discuss putting your dog to sleep in an effort to keep yourselves safe. If your tests come back negative for a brain tumor, do your best to seek answers from other trainers. Pick up the phone and call dog trainers around the country because they might be able to help you determine that there actually is a trigger, and if there is a trigger, the dog is capable of choosing to act aggressively. If your dog is capable of choosing to act aggressively, a good trainer will be able to help you stop this dangerous behavior.

IF YOU ARE CONSIDERING PUTTING your dog to sleep because of common behavioural issues, please reconsider. There is likely to be a shelter, dog rescue or local family who would be willing to adopt your dog and help your dog through these issues. The same can also be said that if your dog has a history of aggression towards other dogs.

REMEMBER that you cannot take back your decision after your dog has been put to sleep, so you'll need to make a decision that keeps you and those around you safe but at the same time is also well thought out. Never put your dog to sleep without seeking all other options and taking enough time to make the right decision. Don't rush the needle, even if your veterinarian wants you to.

WHEN DOG OWNERS call me with dangerous dogs that are bursting with emotion and are ready to put their dog to sleep, I'll try and get them to come in to talk with me in person. Sometimes they are willing to, and other times, something is holding them back. If they are not willing to come in to meet me, I tell them what their options are, and I tell them to get a pen and a piece of paper. On the paper I have them write down two dates and three options.

START BY CHOOSING A DECISION DATE. The decision date should be no more than seven days from today's date. Write down that date on your piece of paper, and agree with your family that you will make a decision on what to do with your dog by that date. The starting date comes next and acts to pinpoint the date that training, rehoming, or euthanization will take place. This date should be no more than three weeks from the decision date. The reason that I suggest this simple exercise is to remind the dog owners that time is ticking.

HERE IS what your paper might look like.

1. Sign up to an extensive dog training program that will get to the root of the issues
2. Rehome your dog or surrender them to a dog rescue or shelter
3. Euthanize your dog

DECISION DATE:_____
    Starting date:_____

EARLIER IN THIS BOOK, I suggested that you should not rush into any decision that will result in your dog being rehomed or put to sleep, but it's important to make these decisions and stick to them on the appointed dates. Why is it so important? Life has a way of getting away from us, doesn't it? I've talked to dozens of dog owners who owned very dangerous dogs that were next to impossible to rehome who took too long to heed my advice. Receiving a call from a frantic dog owner, months after telling them to do something ASAP, is nothing but bone-chilling. "Oh my God Ted. Oh my God, you were right. We should have done something sooner. It's too late now. He attacked my daughter again, and my child will never be the same".

As HARD AS it is to fathom, you will, at some point, be able to forgive yourself for rehoming your dog or putting them to sleep. It may take months, it may take years, but you will rebound. You will not, however, be able to forgive yourself for knowing that something needed to be done in short order, only to have something catastrophic happen a few months later. If your life or the safety of your family is in question, do what you need to do to keep yourself and your family safe.

In RECENT YEARS I've been noticing a disturbing trend with local veterinarians. Some local veterinarians are now refusing to euthanize dogs for any reason if they are healthy. While I agree with this idea in large part, I also think that it should be taken on a case by case with each dog and each owner.

48 HOURS AGO, I had a couple call me who was in a bad position. They had adopted a dog seven months prior because their friend had passed away and none of the local rescues or shelters were willing to step up. This dog was dog and human aggressive but was able to be handled by the couple because she had known the couple since she was a young puppy. As the months went by, her behavior worsened in her new environment, culminating in her biting both a family member and the new owners. The dog also attacked another dog that lived in the building they live in. The male owner is the property manager for the building, and so this puts him in a difficult position. The couple did not even want this dog in the first place, they did not

have money to train the dog properly, and now the male owner was at risk of losing his apartment and job because of this new dog.

He called all of the local animal rescues and shelters again with no luck. His veterinarian refused to euthanize his dog because she was healthy. I hope that this family is ok, I never did hear back from them.

I've heard from other dog owners with dogs that have disfigured the owner's child, yet veterinarians still refuse to put the dog to sleep because the dog is in good health.

For a moment, can we stop worshipping dogs like Gods and realize that we don't live in a perfect world. Many humans avoid training until it's too late, and the dogs are not able to be safely placed in new homes. That's not ideal, but it is the real world. It's my opinion that veterinarians should take each case as an individual in an effort to place the safety and sanity of human beings over that of man's best friend.

# LOOKING AT YOUR OPTIONS

*T*he first thing that you'll want to determine is what your options are moving forward. Will you keep your dog and train them properly? Will you rehome your dog to a new home? Should you seek to surrender to a shelter or animal rescue? Or should you put your dog to sleep? Every family will have a different amount of options, as discussed in the previous chapters in this book.

IF YOU DECIDE to seek help from a quality dog trainer, invest in the best one that you can, and be sure that they will help you get to the root of the problem. Invest wholeheartedly into the training with your time and resources.

IF YOU DECIDE to surrender your dog to a rescue, or shelter, you'll want to be sure to get your up to date on their vaccinations, have them spayed or neutered and acquire their medical records so they can be given to the shelter or rescue. Be sure also to write a letter to your dog's potential adopter to make the transition into a new home easier.

. . .

IF YOU'VE DECIDED to rehome your dog to a new owner, be sure to have your dog spayed or neutered before rehoming them and make sure to have their vaccinations brought up to date. Do research on any potential new adopters to be sure that your dogs will go to a good and loving home, and go and visit the adopters home. Be sure to include their medical records for the new owner and include your dog's life history in a letter to help make the transition easier.

IF YOUR DOG is an imminent threat to your safety or the safety of others, be sure to get some help as soon as you possibly can. Don't delay too long because if you do, you might only have one option, and that's never a good place for dog owners to find themselves.

BEST OF LUCK TO YOU, my heart breaks for you. Feel free to send me an email if you are looking for a trainer in your area, maybe I can find a good match for you. Also, feel free to call me if you need some advice, I get calls from folks around the world in your position, and I'd be more than happy to have a conversation with you to see if I can help.

Ted Efthymiadis
www.tedsbooks.com
ted@tedsbooks.com
902 489 4269


THE END

Made in the USA
San Bernardino, CA
28 February 2020